Answering the Big Questions About God

JIM THOMAS

Cover by Left Coast Design, Portland, Oregon

ANSWERING THE BIG QUESTIONS ABOUT GOD
(formerly *Coffeehouse Theology* and *Streetwise Spirituality*)

Published by Harvest House Publishers
Eugene, Oregon 97402
www.harvesthousepublishers.com

Library of Congress Cataloging-in-Publication Data
Thomas, Jim, 1954–
Answering the big questions about God / Jim Thomas.
p. c.m.
Includes bibliographical references.
ISBN 0-7369-1605-9 (pbk.)
1. Theology, Doctrinal—Popular works. 2. Spirituality. I. Title.
BT77.T453 2005
230—dc22

2004023098

Printed in the United States of America

05 06 07 08 09 10 11 / VP-CF / 10 9 8 7 6 5 4 3 2 1

Contents

Introduction

"No word has been used to reach absolutely opposite concepts as much as the word "god." Consequently, let us not be confused. There is much "spirituality" about us today that would relate itself to the word god or to the idea god; but this is not what we are talking about. Biblical truth and spirituality is not a relationship to the word god, or to the idea god. It is a relationship to the one who is there, which is an entirely different concept."[1]

FRANCIS A. SCHAEFFER

WITH A TITLE LIKE THIS BOOK HAS, I'm aware that many of the following pages ought to be blank. I'm not deluded enough to think I'll be able to answer every question you may have about God. I've even got a few of my own that I have yet to hear a satisfying answer for, and I've got a seminary degree! But the fact that we have questions about a subject as big as God really shouldn't surprise anyone. We are finite and God is infinite. And just by definition that should leave us all standing in awe, with our mouths hanging open, saying the only appropriate thing we could say when thinking about God...*wow!*

To be sure, every author, every public speaker, every vendor of words, expresses himself or herself from the well of personal experience. In talking about spirituality, I'm aware there are as many ideas on the subject as there are people willing to talk about it. Each of us has a starting place. This book reflects what I believe to be a biblical model for spirituality, rooted in the wisdom of the ancient Scriptures and understood through my own experience as

I have walked the path of a Christian pilgrim for more than 40 years.

One of the things I've learned is that a fully integrated life of faith will include the two aspects of *belief* and *experience*. In other words, on one side it will include the truth content of what we say we believe. On the other side, it will include the way we encounter God and live out our faith in everyday life.

I realize some people are drawn to one side more than the other. In this book, my attempt has been to find a balance and not travel so far to one side as to risk ignoring the other. Some of you will wish I had focused more on the experiential side; others, more on the theological content. I hope that, in spite of any imbalance in what follows, God will use the words you find here to encourage you toward a richer and deeper life with Him.

One other item of introduction needs to be mentioned. As a culture, we in the West have replaced the *soul* with the *self*, and the shift toward a "salad bar" spirituality is disturbing. If we can pick and choose what we like about God and just leave the rest, doesn't that mean we're really our own God? How could a God we have designed ever be big enough to deserve our worship, to pray to, or to come to our rescue?

In our deluded narcissism, have we become more interested in being happy than being holy, more interested in being amused and entertained than in bowing before the God who is there or being challenged to respond to Him in loving obedience?

Fortunately, the inescapable fact is that we human beings were created with eternity in our hearts. It's part of our hardware. God created us so that we will always long for a relationship with Him. We will always be drawn to seek Him, to somehow connect with Him and live in a right relationship with Him.

In the pages that follow I will explore spirituality from the perspective of the historic Christian faith, the time-tested faith whose God has rescued my heart and renewed my soul. It is the faith I have embraced with my head and that I awkwardly and inconsistently attempt to live out. But let me emphasize from the beginning that Christian spirituality is not so much about religion or religious actions as it is about an active relationship. It is for all those who live life unceasingly hungry for more, haunted by an insatiable desire for that which lies beyond the reach of this world. It is for those who are spiritually desperate, who have exhausted all the possibilities and achievements they can muster on their own, and who are ready to find renewal for their soul and courage for their heart, all in the simple act of surrender and trust to the God who is there.

- *What does the term* spirituality *really mean?*
- *How does Christian spirituality differ from spirituality in general?*
- *How can we find fulfillment in our spirituality?*

1

What Is Spirituality?

We only know what matter is when spirit dwells in it; we only know what man is when God dwells in him.

William Temple

What Spirituality Is Not

When I first met my wife, she was 15 and I was 19. We were at a church camp called River Valley Ranch in Millers, Maryland, she as a camper, I as the lifeguard. Now, Kim will tell you that for her, it was love at first sight. No, *really*, you can ask her sometime. However, as has often been the case, I was a little slower to "get the message." We were standing outside the camp dining hall along with a hundred other sunburned summer campers, anxiously waiting to get in for some of that delicious and always-nourishing camp food. Kim (who not only gets the message faster than I do, but then goes on to remember minute details surrounding the message longer than I do) tells me I was wearing a trendy pair of brown velvet bell-bottoms, some platform shoes, and a yellow oxford-cloth shirt, and a cleverly coordinated brown velvet bow tie. I know what you are thinking: *What girl* wouldn't *fall instantly in love?*

My point here is not how dashing and debonair I was, but that when I was wearing them, bell-bottoms were "in." However, in the

20-plus years since that fateful week at River Valley Ranch, bell-bottoms have gone in and out of style a couple of times. American culture seems to view clothing and fashion as subject to planned obsolescence. What they told you that you simply must have this year, they tell you that you simply must replace next year. Why? Maybe because we all like new things, but more likely so we can all help whoever "they" are make their condo payments.

It is not just about clothing, though. When I was in high school, "muscle" cars, shag carpet, eight-track tape decks, high-top Converse tennis shoes, the Doobie Brothers, and the Doors were all the rage. (I know, I am really dating myself here.) Thankfully, things have changed a good bit since then. I, for one, was glad to see the demise of shag carpeting and eight-tracks.

These days, it seems that spirituality is popular again. Bookstore shelves are packed with the musings of hundreds of would-be spiritual gurus peddling "new and improved" brands of spirituality and promising that if you buy their books, attend their seminars, and embrace and employ their ideas, you will find spiritual fulfillment. There are as many choices as on the menu of a Chinese restaurant.

Today's spiritualities have some common elements. By and large they are custom-designed to put you in touch with yourself, help you achieve personal happiness, and satisfy your deepest desires for fulfillment. And the wonder of it all is that the new spiritualities ask so very little of you, yet promise so much, if you will only take the time to look within yourself to find the answers.

I have to admit I like the way that sounds. It appeals to many sides of my character. I like new approaches, I love the idea of a free ride with no strings attached, and I *really* like focusing on *me*. But like most people raised in a capitalistic society, and as a thinking person with the last name Thomas (as in "Doubting" Thomas), I am inclined to ask a few questions and harbor a few doubts. Where do these new spiritualities really lead us? To what ultimate source of truth and life are they trying to connect us? Can any spirituality that is so unabashedly self-focused ultimately satisfy us?

Ever the consumers, thousands of us buy into the idea that newer always means better and blindly fall in line behind the next pied-piper mystic that comes along. Why is this so? At least in part because we human beings have the true sense that something important is missing in our lives. We honestly desire to know what it is and how we can find it. Most of us have reached the conclusion that there is more to life than the things we can see, taste, touch, smell, and hear. The deluded optimism of the Enlightenment, which promised that science and human reason could supply us with the answers to all our deepest questions, has now faded. We are left standing in a silent vacuum, listening to the empty echo of our souls, haunted by the unmet desire to know where we have come from, why we are here, and whether we really have a destiny.

But is our only choice to accept a highly suspect, sloganized, "have-it-your-way" spirituality that is trendy, irrational, and subjective? Are we destined to roam from one shallow spiritual fad to another in an endless cycle of novelty and boredom, always seeking but never finding the real thing?

Counterfeit or Real?

You might have heard the story of the incompetent counterfeiter who spent all day making up some funny money. At the end of the day, it dawned on him that he had mistakenly been printing 15-dollar bills. He figured the only way he was going to get anything out of this batch of bills would be to find a place where the people were not too bright and get them to exchange his phony money for real cash.

So he traveled to a small town in the backwoods and went into a little mom-and-pop grocery store. He walked up to the old man behind the counter and asked him, "Do you have change for a 15-dollar bill?"

The old man paused for a second, smiled, and then replied, "I sure do. How would you like that—an eight and a seven, or two sixes and a three?"

That old man was much brighter than the counterfeiter thought he would be. He was alert and aware enough to think critically about what was going on, and this kept him from accepting a counterfeit of the real thing. Had he not been alert, just running on automatic pilot through his sometimes-boring daily life, he could have been fooled by something that, at a casual glance, looked real but would have cost him in the end.

Spirituality as fad or fashion has led many noncritical thinkers to embrace a counterfeit of the real thing. Today's self-focused spiritualities borrow and use the word *soul* when they really mean *self.* At first glance they look like the real thing, but upon further scrutiny it becomes clear where the emphasis lies. We need to understand that a life centered on the self is a counterfeit that will never be satisfying to the soul. A life that fulfills the soul can only be experienced as that life turns upward toward God and outward toward other people.

There is a subtle but significant difference between true spirituality and today's version that focuses on soul massaging and sappy clichés about how "special" we all are. Now don't get me wrong. I do think you are special. And I *know* I am (at least, my mother told me I was). But true spirituality is not just about developing a healthy self-image, losing weight, or improving your inner personal-power skills. True spirituality is about being in a dynamic relationship with God our Creator. It is a fully integrated spiritual life that informs and inspires all other categories of life. True spirituality is not compartmentalized or split off from reality. This is where the Christian faith has much to offer to the discussion of spirituality.

So What *Is* Spirituality?

Do you consider yourself a spiritual person? If so, exactly what does that mean to you?

Different people might answer questions like these in a number of ways. For some, spirituality may be so broad as to include everything from formal religion to massage therapy, astrology, tarot-card readings, meditation, Wicca, the occult, and back-to-nature movements. A discussion of spirituality might include ideas from Eastern mysticism, New Age-ism, and even some of pop psychology's Western optimism. Some would say being a spiritual person just means they believe in God.

Other people might not even include the idea of God in their answer. For them, spirituality means something ethereal and impersonal. Some people would say that being spiritual means they pray from time to time. (*Prayer*—that's one of those spiritual buzzwords that has lost its value through counterfeiting. When people say they pray, I always wonder what they mean. Are they communicating with someone who might actually be listening to their prayers, who might care about what is happening in their lives? Or is prayer for them just wishful thinking and sending out "positive thoughts"?)

There are some people who base their idea of spirituality on an experience they had that gave them an acute sense of a supernatural realm, perhaps an encounter with something they perceived to be an angel, a ghost, a spirit, a demon, or some other such thing. They may have played with a Ouija board, sat in on a séance, or called a psychic hotline. Other people might say they heard the voice of God or the voice of someone who had died. There are even those who have had "near-death experiences." They may have had some kind of accident or illness that caused their heart to stop beating for a moment or two and, during that time, they had an "otherworldly" or "out-of-body" experience in which they saw a bright light, walked through a tunnel, or heard a voice from the heavens.

From the perspective of the Christian faith, we should not dismiss these experiences as totally unreal. There are many instances in the Bible of encounters between the spiritual and earthly realms. People were visited by angels and tormented by demons. God even opened the mouth of a donkey once so it could speak. Understanding the special circumstances and purposes of these events can be enlightening, but that is not my aim here.

Rather, I believe it would be helpful to drop back from any specific and unusual happenings and ask a few questions about the nature of human beings and spirituality. What is it that makes us capable of experiencing the spiritual aspects of life? What part of the human person is it that can sense something beyond the five physical senses? Is spirituality merely intuition, or is it something deeper and more basic to the kind of beings we are? Is our identity, our personhood, limited to our physical body, or is there an immaterial or spiritual aspect to who we are as well?

In the pages that follow, I would like to discuss spirituality from the perspective of historic Christianity. We will search the time-tested ancient Scriptures and the teachings of Jesus for practical help in understanding this mysterious aspect of who and what we are.

Spirituality as a Connection with Someone

In contrast to spirituality as fad and fashion, focused on the self, the historic Christian faith views spirituality as a dynamic relationship in which we commune with God personally, learn to worship God exclusively, and walk in obedience to God with consistency. That kind of relationship stems from a proper understanding of at least three things.

First, Christian spirituality involves an understanding of who God is. This deals with questions such as, Does God really exist, or is He simply a human idea made up to help us feel better about the afterlife? If He does exist, what is He (or It) like? Is He all-powerful? Is He personal or impersonal? Is He loving? Does He care about what happens to us? Is He fair and just? Is God going to one day judge our thoughts and actions?

Second, Christian spirituality involves an understanding of who we are. This area deals with questions such as, What is the nature of the human person? Are we only a physical body, or do we also have a soul? Are we moral creatures, capable of knowing right from wrong? How are we to experience and express our spirituality? What are ways of nurturing our spiritual lives?

Third, Christian spirituality involves an understanding of the relationship that can exist between God and each of us. This deals with questions such as, Can we know God personally? How can we come into a relationship with Him? If He is holy, how can we ever become acceptable to Him? What spiritual disciplines are involved in nurturing a vital relationship with God?

Religions and philosophies can be differentiated by their beliefs about these three issues. Some worldviews hold that God is personal and intelligent; others claim that He (or It) is just an impersonal force that animates the universe. Some worldviews teach that human beings are a product of chance in an impersonal universe; others teach that we are created in the image of God. Some worldviews hold that we can draw near to God; others teach we can only fear Him.

Christian spirituality is about both *belief* and *encounter*. A discussion about Christian spirituality must begin with the understanding that it is rooted in a historic faith that has substance, which is of great value because it means our spiritual experiences are based in and balanced by what we believe to be true about God, ourselves, and other people. The ancient Scriptures serve as the road map to get anywhere within the life of the spirit. One of the primary things they show us is that what we believe about God must also be coupled with a personal *encounter* with Him. As one theologian put it,

> Mere orthodoxy cannot raise dead bones to life. Only God's breath can do that (Ezekiel 37:1-14). We have to taste the goodness of the Lord as well as declare it as a fact. God's love must be poured out into our hearts before we can credibly speak of it with our lips.[1]

This book is about the "how" of Christian spirituality: how we can taste of the goodness of the Lord as we experience and express the life of faith. It is about the spiritual attitudes and disciplines that are necessary if you desire to grow spiritually. You do not have to be a Christian to understand some of what I will say here, but I must tell you that you will not fully understand these things until you are looking at them from the inside. If we are to find the answers to life's deepest questions, if we are to find satisfaction for our deepest longings, it will only be when we humble ourselves and allow ourselves to be arrested by something new, which can only be found in something that is quite old.

Historic Christianity offers unique answers to our questions about spirituality—answers that are not just trendy but life-transforming. This is because the Christian faith does not just lead us to shallow warm and fuzzy feelings, a personality enhancement program, or a set of lifeless religious practices. The Christian faith leads us to a life-changing encounter with the living God.

Whether you consider yourself a person of faith or not, if you have sensed that there is more to life than you are experiencing, that your life is more than just the random movements of a localized conglomeration of flesh, sinew, and bone, hopelessly roaming a dustball-sized planet in a cold and impersonal universe; if you know in your heart that your life is made up of more than the cents' worth of chemicals your physical body is composed of, then I invite you to explore with me the richness of Christian spirituality.

But let me remind you, this is not about "finding yourself." Christian spirituality is about *being found* and rescued by Someone much bigger than you or me. It is about experiencing the God who is there, the infinite and personal God of all creation. That is why Christian spirituality is so thrilling and inexhaustible. That is why, when we live it out with intention, Christian spirituality is always dynamic and never static.

- *Why is it that so many people are unfulfilled in life?*
- *Is this life all there is?*
- *We have more wealth, more entertainment and amusement than any other generation. Why are we so dissatisfied with life?*
- *Is it possible to experience some kind of life that will satisfy us?*

2

Longing: Is This All There Is?

Our lifelong nostalgia, our longing to be re-united with something in the universe from which we now feel cut off, to be on the inside of some door which we have always seen from the outside, is no mere neurotic fancy, but the truest index of our real situation.

C.S. Lewis

Life Is Like a Jigsaw Puzzle

Have you ever felt as though finding fulfillment in life is like trying to assemble a jigsaw puzzle that you cannot ever seem to finish because there is always a piece missing? Just when you think you have it about figured out, with the image starting to come into view, one crucial piece is still missing. Did it fall off the table? Was it eaten by the dog? Is someone playing a cruel joke by stealing pieces when you are not looking? Did someone intentionally package it one piece shy at the factory? Frustrated, you try starting over, thinking next time you will find the missing piece and complete the puzzle. But to make matters worse, each time you try to put it all together, a different piece comes up missing. *Peace, contentment, satisfaction, fulfillment, meaning, purpose*—these are just some of the terms we use to describe those missing pieces.

As I travel around the country, I have heard many people express something similar. Their common sentiment is they feel something is missing in their lives. It is not that they have not achieved significant goals. It is not that they do not have many of the things they thought they wanted. To the contrary, most people acknowledge that this is a great time to be alive. We are the most affluent generation to ever live. We have more disposable income, more high-tech toys, more varieties of entertainment, more access to information than any other culture before us. These things should bring us satisfaction, but somehow they do not. Distraction does not do it. Escape leaves us empty. Amusement cycles back around to boredom. Even religion can leave our soul as dry as a desert.

What is worse, many people have just given up. They have come to the sad conclusion they will never be able to find anything that will satisfy them. They live under a dark cloud of despair, and it seems to them there is little hope of finding a way out from under its suffocating shadow.

Is This All There Is?

Have you ever gone through a period of time when you asked yourself the question, "Is this all there is?" I hope you will find some comfort when I tell you that you are not alone. As a matter of fact, *we* are not alone. I have felt that way, too, and so have millions of other people. We come from all walks of life: rich and poor, educated and uneducated, all races, all religions, all ethnic backgrounds. We are not just tortured authors, poets, artists, and musicians who often feel more than their fair share of angst and despair. We are also public speakers, star baseball players, bank presidents, and preachers. "Is this all there is?" is often asked by the most successful, the most wealthy, and the most famous. They have had a full drink from the well of life. They have tasted all there is of what most of us think might satisfy. But just when they thought they would grasp the golden ring of fulfillment in life, it either slipped through their fingers or crumbled into dust.

A Numbing of the Soul

Every now and then, someone from the celebrity culture gets real enough and honest enough to make an observation that goes against the general worldview of that community. In this excerpt from an interview with actor Brad Pitt in *Rolling Stone* magazine, it is clear that Pitt identifies with the deep longing in the heart of his character "Tyler" from the movie *Fight Club.* (The "Me" is Chris Heath, who was the interviewer.)

> **Pitt:** The point is, the question has to be asked: "What track are we on?" Tyler starts out in the movie saying, "Man, I know all these things are supposed to seem important to us—the car, the condo, our versions of success—but if that's the case, why is the general feeling out there reflecting more impotence and isolation and desperation and loneliness?" If you ask me, I say, "Toss all this, we gotta find something else." Because all I know is that at this point in time, we are heading for a dead end, a numbing of the soul, a complete atrophy of the spiritual being. And I do not want that.
>
> **Me:** So if we're heading toward this kind of existential dead end in society, what do you think should happen?
>
> **Pitt:** Hey, man, I do not have those answers yet. The emphasis now is on success and personal gain. [Smiles] I'm sitting in it, and I'm telling you, that's not it. Whether you want to listen to me or not—and I say that to the reader—that's not it.
>
> **Me:** But, and I'm glad you said it first, people will read your saying that and think...
>
> **Pitt:** I'm the guy who's got everything. I know. But I'm telling you, once you get everything, then you're just left with yourself. I've said it before and I'll say it again: It doesn't help you sleep any better, and you do not wake up any better because of it. Now, no one's going to want to hear that. I understand it. I'm sorry I'm the guy who's got to say it. But I'm telling you.[1]

It can be fairly claimed that when Brad Pitt did this interview, he already had most of what this world has to offer: good looks, youth, fame, and fortune. Pitt has had opportunities that few people will ever get close to in their entire lives. But he has realized something which is profound. In spite of all his wealth and success, life has remained unfulfilling because "once you get everything, then you're just left with yourself." Pitt, too, finds himself wondering if this is all there is.

In the *Pilgrim's Regress*, C.S. Lewis wrote, "What does not satisfy when we find it, was not the thing we were desiring." In other words, many people set out to find satisfaction in things they think hold the key, only to find they have been fooled about which things will truly satisfy their deep desires. We know that becoming a rock star will not be enough. Far too many rock stars have risen to the top professionally, only to crash and burn personally. It is likely that rising to the top of your field will not be enough either. Controlling the lives of your family members will not be enough. Pursuing sexual gratification will not be enough. Being a published author will not be enough. Serving as the pastor of a megachurch will not be enough. This is because our deepest longing is not to be numbered among the privileged, the pleasured, or the powerful. Those are the distractions, the decoys we chase while thinking we are in pursuit of the real thing. It is not that there is anything wrong with those things when they are put in their proper place. It is just that they will not ultimately satisfy our deepest longings.

The principle is that nothing finite will ultimately satisfy the deep yearning in our hearts. Opportunities will not satisfy, pleasure will not satisfy, significance will not satisfy. Even reading a book on the subject of spirituality (this one included) will not satisfy the restlessness and longing that haunts our souls.

What I Am Looking For

Several years back, the band U2 had a worldwide hit song entitled "I Still Haven't Found What I'm Looking For." One of the reasons it was so popular was because it struck a chord in the hearts of many people. The message was basically this: *I've been a lot of places, seen a lot of things, and done a lot of things. But in spite of all that, I feel alienated. Life remains unfulfilling and still seems hopeless. I really want to find what it is that will turn things around for me.* The band came up with a great arrangement, and Bono, the band's vocalist, delivered the message with an honesty and passion that resonates with anyone who has ever felt this deep longing and wondered whether life could somehow become meaningful.

Today, millions of people have not found what they are looking for either. Worse, many do not even know what the "what" is that they should be looking for. For many people, just living everyday life is like stumbling around with a ball and chain tied to their soul. Just getting out of bed stirs up questions like, What's the point? Who cares? Why bother?

The French existentialist philosopher Jean-Paul Sartre once said, "A finite point has no meaning unless it has an infinite reference point." There is a sense in which Christian teaching agrees with Sartre, in that human beings are like a finite point. Our lives are contingent; we are not the source of our own being, and we do not sustain ourselves by our own power. We are dependent on many other things simply to exist, to breathe, and to eat, let alone to find meaning in life. When we try to find fulfillment in the finite, we are like a dog chasing its tail. Every now and then we will think we have succeeded in catching fulfillment, but we have to bite down pretty hard to keep it, and then all we have achieved is sinking our teeth into our finite selves. Not only is the accomplishment disappointing, but it is likely to leave us in a great deal of pain.

Sartre was right about the meaninglessness of existence for a finite point without an infinite reference point. Sadly, Sartre was an atheist, so he himself recognized no infinite reference point. Life for him was ultimately meaningless and absurd. While we might commend him for his insightful analogy and his brutal honesty, this does not mean we must agree with his conclusion about whether there is an infinite reference point.

The answer to Brad Pitt's longing, the answer to U2's longing, the answer to Sartre's longing, the answer to your longing and my longing is all the same. We are all looking for something infinite that can serve as a reference point for our finite lives. Is there such an infinite reference point? If so, where can it be found?

Looking for the Infinite Reference Point

There is a village community on the panhandle of Florida called Seaside, which attracts people who enjoy getting away from it all. My wife and I like to go there to reflect, write, and rest. We have a little routine we enjoy, which includes an early-morning walk on the beach, followed by a period of sitting under an umbrella in our beach chairs for some reading and quiet. Then when the crowd swells, Kim and I head back to our cottage for some writing and more reading, and she might pick up her paintbrush and toy with a visual image or two.

In the late afternoon, after the crowds have had their fill of sand and sun, we gather up our beach chairs and head back down to the shoreline for a walk in the dusk and some sunset reading. It is not unusual for us to be sitting in our chairs, staring into the horizon, as the sun disappears down the western end of the white-sand beach. In the quiet of those moments, we can experience something gigantic and truly wonderful. We can look out into the ocean, then look harder and farther out, and still not see the end of it all. Fishing boats shrink to the size of gnats, navy battleships disappear into the vast beyond. I know it is not infinite—the ocean holds just so much water—but there is something immense about it that quiets the human heart and reminds us that there is more.

In addition to the visual feast, I also love the rhythm of the surf on the sand as it rolls in and out. The relentless lumbering of the waves, each one sent from some secret origin, reminds me of the beauty and order of the physical universe. I suppose I am something of a paradox, in that I am drawn at the same time by both permanence and change. There is something permanent and anchoring about the hugeness of the ocean, but something new and refreshing about each incoming wave.

Sitting by the ocean can give our souls a temporary oasis, a place to rest and settle down. I could speak the same way about other places that move me similarly: Puget Sound in the Pacific Northwest, the island of Kauai, and the Côte d'Azur of southern France.

But as wonderful as it is, even if we moved to Seaside permanently, I would soon discover the deepest longing in my soul coming to the surface again, in the same way the missing puzzle piece makes its absence known. The good things of this world—the ocean, the mountains, the rivers, and the valleys—provide us with a resting place that is only temporary. As vast and beautiful as they are, we soon discover they are not the thing we are really looking for. While we can appreciate them, we cannot commune with them. They are simply road signs to point us in the direction of the one thing that will ultimately satisfy our soul's longing. C.S. Lewis comments:

> The books or the music in which we thought the beauty was located will betray us if we trust to them; it was not *in* them, it only comes *through* them, and what came through them was longing. These things—the beauty, the memory of our own past—are good images of what we really desire; but if they are mistaken for the thing itself they turn into dumb idols, breaking the hearts of their worshipers. For they are not the thing itself; they are only the scent of a flower we have not found, the echo of a tune we have not heard, news from a country we have not visited.[2]

One of the wisest men to ever walk the planet was a Jewish monarch named Solomon, who lived about 3000 years ago. Solomon had everything anyone could ever want. He had more riches, pleasure, and power than he could enjoy, even if he had lived a hundred lifetimes. But in his old age, as Solomon was reflecting on the course of his life, he became quite melancholy, and it is likely this was when he wrote the book called Ecclesiastes, found in the Old Testament of the Bible.

In Ecclesiastes, Solomon dons the name *Qoheleth*, which is Hebrew for "teacher," and the message he passes on to his student readers comes through loud and clear. More than 30 times he refers to life and its experiences as a cycle of emptiness and "vanity." He reminds us that all pleasure, projects, property, and power are vanity. All human understanding and undertakings are vanity. He views all human tragedy, pain, grief, and suffering as meaningless. From beginning to end, and all the way in between, Solomon came to the conclusion that mankind is powerless and blind, unable to make any sense whatsoever of life. "All is vanity and striving after wind" serves as the repeated summary statement throughout the book. But there is also some incredible hope to be found in this book. In chapter 3, Solomon makes the statement that God has set *eternity* in our hearts. This is an amazing claim because it reveals that although we are finite creatures, God has given us the capacity to connect with the infinite. This is why we all feel such deep-seated longing inside us. As Augustine said, "Longing makes the heart deep," and spiritual yearning is born out of the possibility of connecting that God has placed within us. When we find life's finite experiences to be less-than-satisfying, there is nothing wrong with us. We are just experiencing, indirectly, the awareness of eternity with which God has made us. The great news is that God has much more in store for us than this broken and polluted world will ever be able to provide. "God's beautiful but tantalizing world is too big for us, yet its satisfactions are too small. Since we were made for eternity, the things of time cannot fully and permanently satisfy," remarks Derek Kidner.

I highly recommend you read Ecclesiastes, but please do not read it slowly. Read the entire book in one sitting, or you may find yourself ready to give up on everything! On the surface, the mood is somber. Qoheleth writes viscerally, and if you are given to melancholy, he will take you to the edge of the abyss. But the Teacher does not leave us without hope. Toward the end of this powerfully honest book, Solomon draws a contrast between two ways of thinking about life. He calls one "folly" and the other "wisdom," and then moves on to show us which path leads to wisdom. In chapters 10 through 12 he makes a transition from the tough realities of despair to the source of hope, and he shows us where we can look for a solution. If our lives are to have any meaning whatsoever, we will need to live courageously and joyfully, and Solomon tells us this can only happen if we learn to trust, fear, and obey our Creator.

This is the beginning point of Christian spirituality. We must recognize that the longing we feel arises because we live in a finite universe that simply cannot offer the satisfaction we are looking for. This longing is haunting and relentless. It will not be silenced by the noise, busyness, and obsessive productivity of contemporary life. But we are not left without an answer.

Christian spirituality points us to the infinite reference point, and the great news is that this infinite reference point is not a "what" or an "it." It is a "who." This infinite reference point is not an impersonal force or fate, but a God with a face. This is the God who calls us to Himself to be in relationship with Him. When we commune with God, He in return communes with us in a way that the rest of created nature simply cannot. As our Creator, He is able to touch our souls, to speak to us, to satisfy the deep longing that churns in our hearts. And ultimately, God's answer is to move us from longing to belonging.

- *Are we all alone in the universe?*
- *Doesn't everyone belong to God?*
- *Is being a Christian just about believing certain things, or is there more to it than that?*
- *How can we have a meaningful relationship with God?*

3

Belonging: Am I All Alone in the Universe?

The greatest honor we can give Almighty God is to live gladly because of the knowledge of his love.

JULIAN OF NORWICH

Designed for Relationship

I recently heard a report about a middle-aged woman who jumped out the window of her fourteenth-floor apartment. Just a couple of minutes before her death, a man washing windows on the outside of a nearby building had greeted her, and they had exchanged smiles. Then when he turned his back, she jumped.

She left a note in her apartment that read, "I can't endure one more day of this loneliness. My phone never rings. I never get letters. I don't have any friends!" Ironically, a neighbor who lived just across the hall told reporters, "I wish I had known she felt so lonely. I'm lonesome myself."[1] Have you ever had a deep feeling of loneliness? Have you ever felt isolated, disconnected, or alienated in life? Psychologists have suggested there is an epidemic of loneliness in our culture. For some reason, more and more people are complaining that they feel estranged and isolated.

Interestingly, we have more and better access to each other than ever before. We have cell phones, videophones, digital pagers, wireless e-mail, and a host of other ways of staying in touch. You would think we would feel more connected and less lonely now than at any other time in the history of the world. Yet, have you noticed how it can ruin some people's day to come home and find there are no messages on the answering machine, or when they go on-line and do not hear those three little words: "You've got mail"?

Someone has said that loneliness is more than just being alone. There is a cold isolation, a hollow silence in the soul when a person is longing for relationship but has no one to turn to. While many people enjoy seasons of solitude, nobody does well when being alone is his or her only option. Loneliness can suck the life right out of a human soul because we have been created with personality, and personality thrives on relationships, and without healthy relationships, the human soul languishes.

Contrary to popular myth, loneliness is not reserved for single people. There are many married people who live a lonely existence because their obsession with busyness leaves them with no time to either enjoy the relationships they do have or develop any new ones. Other married people might have a workaholic spouse or a cold and indifferent one. Lonely people live in any number of settings. They might be in a major metropolitan city, walking the streets daily, surrounded by thousands of people, and still feel left out. They can be sitting in a crowded restaurant, circled about by fellow workers and acquaintances, but still have that gnawing sense that when it gets right down to it, they live a disconnected life.

Loneliness has led many people to depression and some to despair. This is because we measure our lives by the vitality of our relationships. If our relationships are mostly nonexistent or troubled, we are left with hollow hearts. If our relationships are vibrant, our soul can seem full. The condition of our closest relationships will affect us most deeply. When you are at odds with someone you see every day, like a fellow worker, it can be upsetting. But when you are at odds with someone you live with, like your spouse or children, it can be disastrous.

On the most intimate level, in the deepest part of our souls, we are never more alone than when we are at odds with God. Because they are spiritual orphans, those people living without a personal relationship with God struggle with the horrible sense that they are all alone in the universe, with no sense of why they are alive, why they feel left out, or what to do about it all.

The Fuel Our Souls Run On

It is very important for us to evaluate our ideas about God if we are to ever discover a meaningful and fulfilling spiritual life. C.S. Lewis put it this way: "God designed the human machine to run on himself. He himself is the fuel our spirits were designed to burn, or the food our spirits were designed to feed on. There is no other. That is why it is just no good asking God to make us happy in our own way."[2] False ideas about who God is will only take us further down the road to spiritual emptiness, frustration, and disappointment.

In this vein, William Temple commented, "If your conception of God is radically false, then the more devout you are, the worse it will be for you. You are opening your soul to be molded by something base. You had much better be an atheist."[3] And so, if we recognize that we are spiritual beings, if we believe in God and express any kind of devotion to God, it becomes vitally important that we focus our spiritual attention on the God who is really there, rather than on a god we have imagined or come up with on our own.

The God with Personality

Christian spirituality centers on the idea of *belonging* to God, of coming into a deep relationship with the God who is infinite and personal. This would not be possible if God were an impersonal force or fate. In his book *True Spirituality*, Francis Schaeffer confirms that "all the reality of Christianity rests upon the reality of the existence of a personal God." What does Christianity mean when it says that God is personal? It means that God has the quality of being a particular personality, as opposed to being an impersonal energy or life force. God is personal, not in the sense that each of us has our own personal god who exists to serve as our private magic genie, divine puppet, or cosmic concierge, but in that God is who He is. He is not simply who any one of us might understand Him to be. God is not subject to human imagination. Recognizing this changes everything.

God is a being who has intelligence, awareness, and real personality. In the New Testament (Matthew 6:9-13) we find the record of what is commonly called the "Lord's Prayer." The first few phrases of this prayer speak loudly and clearly of the personality of God. Jesus said we are to address God as "our Father." This clearly tells us that God has personality. A father is a person and is capable of relationship. We are to say to God our Father, "Hallowed be Your name," implying we worship a God who is a Person, who has a name. "Your kingdom come" tells us that this personal God is also the sovereign Ruler over His kingdom and can exercise His rule. "Your will be done" tells us that God has a will, therefore He has a mind, an agenda, and is self-determined. This is just one of many examples of how the Christian idea of God embraces the fact that God is personal.

Ownership Versus Relationship

Christian spirituality focuses on the God who has designed and created you and me and everything that exists, and the Scriptures reveal that God has built into our software the capacity to have a relationship with Him. There is a popular notion that says we all belong to God and are all God's children, and in one sense the Bible would agree. Deuteronomy 10:14 (NIV) tells us, "to the LORD your God *belong* the heavens, even the highest heavens, the earth and everything in it" (emphasis added). That pretty much covers all of creation.

Since God has made everything that exists, everything does belong to God. But this is belonging primarily in terms of ownership. Christian spirituality carries with it the idea that God has offered us the opportunity to move from ownership to relationship. My wife and I love each other dearly, even to the point of saying we belong to each other. But ours is not a belonging of ownership. It is a belonging of relationship, of devotion, of willful commitment and deep trust. Because we have come into this deeply intimate relationship, we have moved from loneliness and longing to belonging on a human level.

When we turn to the issue of spirituality, how do we come into that kind of intimate relationship with God? How do we move from mere existence and ownership to a thriving and personal relationship? Can a person move from his or her deep spiritual longing for God to fully belonging to God? The Christian idea of spirituality says yes.

Dealing with the Separation

The Christian faith teaches that we are all sinners, and therefore we are all separated from God. This separation is at the root of our sense that something is missing. It is why we are haunted by such a deep longing. It is why we ask the question, "Is this all there is?" We feel separated from the very Source of life because our sin has put up a barrier between us and God. Whether or not we know it, what we all long for is to be back in a right relationship with God. While this separation from Him is real, the Scriptures also teach us that God has graciously made a way to bridge the gap that separates us from Him. Christ came and paid the price to ransom us from sin, and because of His death on the cross that ransoms us, when we place our trust in Him the separation between us and God is removed. God did not owe it to us to make a way for us to come back to Him. It is not something we deserve in any way at all. God has simply done it, and the Bible tells us that the reason God did it was because of His immense love for us.

Our part in dealing with the separation is to respond by recognizing our need for God and His free gift of salvation, and to turn from our sin and bow before Him. We can't work our way into heaven or into God's good graces. His forgiveness cannot be achieved; it must simply be received. We cannot tip the balance of the moral scales in our own favor. None of us are good enough for that. The only way to deal with our sin is for it to be forgiven. We begin by admitting our spiritual bankruptcy and powerlessness. We cry out for God's help, and the Bible tells us that all who call on the name of the Lord will be saved. Realizing that you cannot save yourself and placing your trust in Christ, who died for your sin, is the starting point of a life of Christian spirituality.

From Longing to Belonging

When you become a Christian, you take the first step to achieving true spiritual satisfaction because, at that point, God moves you from your place of longing to a place of belonging. You move from being alone with yourself in the universe to having a relationship with the infinite, personal God.

There are many concepts of spirituality that take a completely different route to an altogether different destination. They will sometimes borrow Christian terms, but they actually mean nothing by them. The word *god* or the word *faith* can be superficial or nebulous when employed simply to give a gloss of religious legitimacy to what is in reality empty rhetoric. In the end, if a concept of God or spirituality leads people back around to themselves or to an impersonal or vague concept of God, it will eventually leave them empty and wanting more. The self can never fill the soul. It is in God alone that we find the answer to our soul's longing. Augustine put it this way: "You [God] have made us for yourself, and our hearts will be restless until we find our rest in you."

The truth and reality of Christian spirituality give your existence meaning because they declare that your life is about more than just you, or the things you own and the things you do. Once you are a Christian, you belong to the God who is a Someone. You belong in a deep and intimate way, not just by ownership but by relationship. Christian spirituality is not just about church attendance or membership. It is about citizenship in a heavenly kingdom and being in relationship with the heavenly King. Once you become a Christian, you are transferred from the kingdom of self to the kingdom of God, from the kingdom of darkness to the kingdom of light.

And there is more good news: It is not based on your performance. You cannot move from longing to belonging by being good enough, by praying long enough, by going to church enough, or by doing (or not doing) anything enough. It is only by God's gift that we can enter into this relationship with Him. We put our trust in Christ, we trust that what He did when He died on the cross was enough to bring us back to God, and then God moves us from mere ownership to personal relationship. God has taken the initiative, and now we cannot only know *about* Him, but we can actually know Him.

The first time a person becomes truly aware of this, it is as if a light goes on inside, and all of a sudden everything in life looks different. As the old hymn says, "I once was lost, but now am found, was blind, but now I see." To many people, God reveals Himself in a subtle and most intimate way, and they are drawn into an initial encounter with Him. God may arrange that they encounter Him during some pleasant experience, while down at the beach, up on a mountain, riding a bike, or walking in a garden. Other people have found themselves in a situation where they have come to the end of their rope and run out of their own self-sufficiency. Recognizing their need, they desperately turn to God, only to find that He was already there, waiting for them, arranging the whole thing so they would meet Him personally.

God comes and reveals Himself to a person in as many ways as we might be able to imagine. In each case, the encounter is authored by Him, and as author Brennan Manning has said, it is then we are "seized by the power of a great affection." The strong grip of God's love and grace brings us into the most secure form of belonging possible, because God has promised that He will never leave us or forsake us.

A Growing Knowledge of God

Belonging to God also includes the idea of our having a hunger to grow in our knowledge of Him. Once we have come to know the Lord, we are naturally interested in getting to know Him better. That is the way it is with anyone that we truly like or love. We want to spend time with that person. We want to get to know them better. How can we do this? God has revealed Himself through the written word of the Scriptures and through Jesus Christ, the living Word, who became a human being. We can begin to search the Scriptures and find out what God is like, what pleases Him, and how He wants us to live out our relationship with Him. We can also look at the life of Jesus and learn about God in a more direct way. What did Jesus think about love, poverty, wealth, marriage, and telling the truth? What did Jesus think about holiness and hypocrisy? The answers to these questions are found in the New Testament, which makes available to us a credible knowledge of God.

This always-growing knowledge of God deepens our sense of belonging and provides us with an anchor for our life of faith. Christians believe in God, but we also believe some very specific things about God and about the relationship between God, humanity, and the rest of creation. These beliefs have been summarized in the historic creeds of the church. These beliefs are foundational and they nurture a steadfast, growing faith.

But belonging to God is not just a matter of head knowledge. It also includes a relationship with Him that we experience from day to day as we respond to Him by worshiping, obeying, and serving from a heart filled with gratitude for what He has given us. It is not just about the initial step of getting "saved." As author and philosopher Dallas Willard has pointed out, following Jesus is not just about "sin management." It is not just about securing our eternal life insurance or having our sin dealt with on the legal and eternal end of things. Although those things are important and are the beginning point, we are also called to become *disciples* of Jesus Christ. We are called to follow Christ, to walk in a daily relationship with God by the power of the Holy Spirit, who lives in every believer.

The Scriptures describe our spiritual belonging as experiential. First Peter 2:9 (NIV) tells us, "You are a chosen people, a royal priesthood, a holy nation, a people belonging to God, that you may declare the praises of him who called you out of darkness into his wonderful light." Jesus says in John 8:47 (NIV), "He who belongs to God hears what God says. The reason you do not hear is that you do not belong to God."

If you write and teach about theology as I do, it is sometimes easy to forget the importance of belonging. But we must not reduce our study of God to a scientific system or a ritualized religion. God is not some*thing* we study, He is Some*one* we are in relationship with. God is Someone who loves us and Someone we can express love back to. God has made it possible for you and me to *belong* to Him as far more than mere possessions. In the deepest part of our souls, there is an empty place that can only be filled when we realize that we belong to God and then go about living in a personal relationship with Him. Belonging to God in this way is the answer to our deepest longing.

In his classic book *The Pursuit of God*, A.W. Tozer sums it up concisely:

> When religion has said its last word, there is little that we need other than God Himself. The evil habit of seeking God-*and* effectively prevents us from finding God in full revelation. In the "and" lies our great woe. If we omit the "and," we shall soon find God, and in Him we shall find that for which we have all our lives been secretly longing.[4]

- *If truth exists, how do we come to know or believe it when we see it?*
- *What is the difference between belief and knowledge?*
- *Is there such a thing as religious truth?*
- *Can we really know anything with certainty?*
- *How do we come to a knowledge of God?*
- *Can we really know anything about God?*
- *What is the relationship between faith and reason?*

4

What Is the Difference Between Belief and Knowledge?

If we submit everything to reason, our religion will have no mysterious and supernatural element. If we offend the principles of reason, our religion will be absurd and ridiculous.

BLAISE PASCAL, *Pensées,*

Peekaboo

One of the things I like about traveling is getting the opportunity to "people watch." There are so many interesting people around the country, and not the least of these are the many wide-eyed toddlers we encounter in airports. On one particular occasion while sitting at a gate in the Atlanta airport, a young mother and her two children sat just across the way from me. One of her kids looked to be a little over a year old. He was a cute little fellow and just full of personality. The minute our eyes met we both beamed with excitement. *Ahhh!* I thought. *Someone else who loves life!*

From that initial contact we deepened our relationship by moving into a round of peekaboo. Peekaboo is a great game. It is so portable and inexpensive. All you need are two excitable faces and something to hide them behind. You can use a newspaper, the corner of a hallway, some lady's beehive hairdo, or just your own two hands. And so we peeked and booed a couple of times, laughing out loud and having a great time. But then this little fellow did something I had not seen before. He closed his eyes, hung his head down and got real still for about 15 seconds.

At first, I was not quite sure what this meant. But then I figured out that he thought if he closed *his* eyes, since he was not seeing me, then I could not see him either. If it was dark to him, then it was dark to everyone.

But in spite of what my fun-loving younger friend believed, the reality was that I could in fact see him, because he was still there. I did not have my eyes shut. It was not dark for me, and I was looking straight at him.

Youthful naïveté cannot eclipse reality.

Superman

Perhaps you have heard the story of the professional wrestler who got on board an airplane and sat down in the first-class section. He was tall, good-looking, and muscular, a self-assured man dressed in black leather accented with lots of gold chains.

Once everyone got on board and found their seats, the flight attendant closed the hatch and started down the aisle to make sure everyone was ready for takeoff. When she came to the wrestler, she stopped and asked, "Sir, would you mind fastening your seat belt?" to which the cocky athlete retorted, "Honey, Superman don't need no seat belt!"

A ripple of chuckles spread through those seated nearby.

Then she, being sharp of mind and quick of wit, responded with, "All due respect, sir, but *Superman* don't need no airplane."

Clearly the professional wrestler was not faster than a speeding bullet, more powerful than a locomotive, or able to leap over tall buildings in a single bound. He was not the famed man of steel he fancied himself to be. He was probably just guilty of buying into what his publicist had been saying about him.

But deluded self-confidence and hype cannot eclipse reality.

How We Think

All of this goes to show that what we choose to believe may not always be true to reality. As the world becomes increasingly interconnected, with a free flow of ideas shared across cultural lines, it becomes more important than ever for us to have a way to evaluate the truth and falsity of conflicting viewpoints. If one person has grown up believing that the world is flat and someone else comes along and says, "No, it is round," it is a good thing for somebody to get into a boat and set sail to pursue the matter further, to find out which viewpoint is true to reality.

If you and I are to be good thinkers and informed people, we should evaluate *how* we think. Are we thinking clearly? Are the methods we use to determine what is true, what is real, and what can be rationally believed valid? And how does religion fit into the discussion of knowledge and belief? Are there places where faith and reason intersect? Do some religious belief systems line up with reason more closely than others?

If we want to determine what is true and what is false in the area of religious belief, we must first understand a little about the process of how we come to know and believe anything at all. Since this can turn into a bit of a brain-twister, you might want to grab a highly caffeinated beverage, sit up in your chair, and get ready to dig in.

How We Know

Epistemology sounds like one of those words you should never mention at the dinner table. It is the term philosophers use to discuss the origin, nature, and limits of human knowledge. Epistemology deals with questions like, What can we know? How do we come to know anything? What is the difference between belief and knowledge? How can we come to know or believe anything with certainty?

The cultural melting pot we now live in brings together ideas and values from many sources and offers some wonderful benefits. But it has also prompted a crisis over issues like truth, morality, and shared values. For example, while most people agree that "family values" are important, there is no longer a consensus in our culture about what the term "family values" really means. And as soon as anyone begins to offer a definition, another person raises up a list of exceptions, usually accompanied by the statement, "Who are *you* to push *your* values on *me?*" The result is a culture frozen in moral stalemate, impotent to speak with clarity on difficult moral issues like the teaching of ethics in our school systems, how to deal with violent criminals, how to go about eliminating racism, and how to handle issues like abortion and euthanasia.

This increasing moral confusion is an example of why epistemology is such an important category of thought. We have lost our moral consensus because we have lost sight of objective truth on a cultural level. People do not know what they can believe anymore. And we are quickly losing sight of objective truth on the individual level as well. Every day we read another example of how someone asked all the big questions of life and came up with the wrong answers. "Is there meaning to life? Are there consequences to my actions? Is there such a thing as right or wrong?" If the answer to these questions is "no, no, and no," who can blame people for wanting to smash and destroy? Who can blame them for wanting to end it all? They are simply dealing with what they perceive to be the painful truth of their meaningless lives in an honest way.

But there really is a better way. According to the Bible, the answer to those big questions is not "no." It is "yes, yes, and yes." The Christian faith teaches that there is real meaning to life, every human life is significant, there are consequences to our actions, and there is such a thing as right and wrong.

As rational creatures we think and form opinions, sometimes consciously, sometimes unconsciously. But as G. K. Chesterton once said, "A man who refuses to have his own philosophy will only have the used-up scraps of somebody else's philosophy." So if we are to take thinking seriously, we need to consider how we determine which beliefs are true. Whether talking about simple things like how much air pressure is right for my tires or complex things like the meaning of life, arriving at the truth should always be the goal. And while macaroni and cheese is a fairly simple meal, and chicken tikka masala is a bit more complicated, so too, some categories of philosophy are simple and others are quite complicated. Epistemology can be a bit of both, but it does offer us a chance to evaluate how we think and how we come to belief and knowledge.

Simple and Complex Truth

The story has been told that there was once a football coach at a major university who was trying to get a rather dense football player through a math exam which he had flunked once already. So the coach went to the professor and said, "Professor, if this student can't pass math, he can't play football. And we really need him on the team. Would you please give him another chance?" The professor was supportive of the football program at the university, and so he agreed to test the student one more time.

They called the student in. The professor, now fully determined to see him pass the test, said, "I'm going to ask you just one question. If you answer it correctly, you'll pass the exam and can play football." He then asked the student, "What is two times six?" The young man thought for a moment, and then finally he smiled real big and said, "Two times six is twelve!"

The professor smiled, too. But then to the professor's horror, the coach approached him and pleaded, "Uh, professor...could you give him just one more chance?"

That story shows us that some categories of knowledge involve simple, logical truth, and mathematics is perhaps the most obvious of these. In spite of the coach's ignorance, two times six always has been and always will be twelve. There are other areas of physical science which deal with simple, logical truth as well. For example, we can know with some certainty that water at sea level will boil at 212°F or 100°C. This is a repeatable experiment that shows little to no variance. We can say we know its outcome with great certainty.

But there are also more complicated truths that most people readily embrace. These include propositional statements from the categories of science, history, philosophy, and religion. For instance, the theory of relativity, carbon-14 dating of archaeological artifacts, the uniqueness of each self-conscious individual, and belief in the existence of God are more complicated truths, but nonetheless truths most people believe with some amount of certainty.

Poetical Truth

In addition to logical truth, there is also what some people have called "poetical" truth, which we find more often in the fine arts. This can be found when someone makes up a story which, though fictional, has some aspects of reality to it. There may be names and places that correspond to the real world, but in essence the entire thing is fiction: a parable, a myth, a fable, or a fantasy. While there may be a good moral principle we can draw out of the story, its details are not to be taken as logically true.

Truth in Religion

When it comes to religion, you will find propositional statements that contain both logical and poetic truths. Some people make the mistake of thinking all religious truth is poetic truth, that it is all parable and allegory, and that it can mean whatever each person might want it to mean. But that is simply not the case. Most religions assert propositional statements of logical truth, and when they do, those propositions should be subject to the law of noncontradiction. No clearly contradictory statements of logical truth can both be true at the same time and in the same relationship. So whenever we are talking about logical truth claims, even in the area of religious truth, the law of noncontradiction still holds.

Still with me? (Now would be an excellent time to pause, take a deep breath, and sip your highly caffeinated beverage.)

Testing the Truth of Religion

At this point someone might ask, "Then how can we really know for sure? How can we test religious truth claims?" I believe we should treat logical truth statements the same way in all categories of thought. By that I mean that as much as we believe the mathematical truth that two times six is twelve and the historical truth that "George Washington was the first president of the United States of America," we can similarly evaluate statements about religious truth and come to some rational conclusions about their truthfulness.

For instance, if a religious truth claim contradicts an established truth from the area of science, history, or philosophy, then that religious truth claim becomes suspect. Please note that I said "an *established* truth" as a qualifier. If a religion were to claim that human beings could fly unaided, that religion would have a long way to go before we should take it seriously because it is a well-established truth that human beings cannot fly unaided.

Let's look at a more realistic example. Judaism, Christianity, and Islam all believe that the universe had a beginning, that it was created by an intelligent, supernatural Deity. If it could be proved beyond a shadow of a doubt that the universe has always existed and never had a beginning, then this fundamental truth claim of all three major religions would be in question. But since that is not the case, these three religions have not been proven false on their common viewpoint about the origin of the universe (if anything, science continues to discover more credible evidence pointing to the idea that the universe did indeed have a beginning).

Judaism, Islam, and Christianity believe quite differently when it comes to other logical truth claims, however, especially those about Jesus Christ. Judaism and Islam would agree that Jesus existed and was a moral teacher. They would even go so far as to say He was a prophet. But they would never admit to His resurrection.

Christianity, on the other hand, claims that Jesus was the very Son of God and that He rose from the dead in space-time history. There is a clear contradiction between these propositional truth statements, and they cannot both be true. Either Jesus rose from the dead or He did not. If He did not, then the case for Christianity is greatly weakened. If He did, then Christianity has an incredible hope to offer the world.

What Is Believable?

The way to decide whether any proposition is believable is to assemble the evidence and employ reason. This is the same way a criminal court gets to the truth about whether or not someone has committed a crime. There may be overwhelming evidence which puts the accused person at the scene of the crime at just the right time, and also shows the person to have had proper motive. This evidence might include a gun with the defendant's fingerprints all over it, or some other forensic evidence, like a footprint, hair, or blood. Even though the defendant claims to be innocent and there were no eyewitnesses present, the jury may still conclude that the defendant is guilty based on the amount of convincing evidence.

Working together with reason and logic, that evidence can persuade a jury to bring a conviction in the matter. If someone is deemed guilty, the judgment is described as "guilty, beyond a reasonable doubt" or "guilty, based on a preponderance of the evidence."

Someone might say, "Yeah, but that's not knowing beyond all doubt. Juries make mistakes; sometimes the wrong guy goes to jail." Fair enough, but to operate in the real world, on a day-to-day basis, we cannot have a bunch of people running around loose in society who we are 99.9 percent sure are thieves, murderers, and rapists.

To coexist in relative peace, when we see something that walks like a duck, talks like a duck, and lays duck eggs, we can indeed come to the conclusion that it is not a mule. It is indeed a duck. As a wise man once pointed out, "We must believe something before we can know anything."

The Difference Between Belief and Knowledge

I was corresponding with a professor of psychology from a major university once, and he confessed that he was wrestling with some of the intellectual and existential aspects of religious belief. He had become a Christian early on in life but, after years of working in an increasingly naturalistic educational system, he had come to a crisis in his beliefs. It was clear to me that he had questions on his mind and longings in his heart, so I encouraged him to know that his honest doubts were not a violation of belief, that he was not doing something wrong in God's eyes by asking questions about issues of faith. On the contrary, doubt can be a sign that a person is actively engaged in thinking.

The central issue running through most of his questions revealed that he seemed to equate what we can *know* with what we may *believe.* But they are not the same.

Knowledge, as most people use the term, relies exclusively on observation and experience. It involves raw data coming into the mind through the five senses. Through knowledge we conclude that ice is cold, water is wet, and fire is hot. This data may be evaluated based on other empirical information previously stored in the mind as well, but the instant there is any kind of value judgment involved, we have moved from knowledge to belief. (Knowledge is the centerpiece of *empiricism,* the viewpoint which claims "seeing is believing" and that direct knowledge is the only real knowledge. The weakness of empiricism is that it would have to exclude knowledge of things we cannot taste, touch, smell, hear, or see, such as magnetism, gravity, wind, electricity, love, hope, justice, or goodness. And ultimately, the principle "seeing is believing" would have to be excluded from empiricism as well, as it is a concept and not something one can "see.")

Belief relies on observation and experience, but it also adds the element of common sense based on human reason. Belief involves raw data coming in through the five senses, which is then organized by human reasoning, evaluated for credibility, discerned morally, and then, in the end, judged by a person's common sense. Belief involves the senses, the mind, the will, and the heart of a person. They work together to convince us that something is true.

There are varying degrees of conviction in our beliefs. These sometimes fluctuate, but ultimately we choose, either actively or passively, what we will believe. Of course, what we choose to believe does not in any way affect the nature of reality. We might very well believe things which are not true. Whether you believe in God or not does not alter whether or not God *actually* exists. But for the rational person, the goal would be to discover and believe those things which are true, those things which correspond with reality.

Knowledge and belief show up in many areas of our lives. I *know* there is a car parked in my driveway. But I *believe* that love between two people is something that is real, even though it is often unpredictable and not as verifiable or consistent. I *know* that fire is hot, but I *believe* that murder is morally wrong.

In the sense in which I have defined the terms, belief is deeper than knowledge because belief involves more human faculties than knowledge does. This does not mean that belief and knowledge must stand opposite and against each other. To the contrary, to get to the truth in a matter, especially matters of faith, they must stand side by side. As Blaise Pascal said, "Faith indeed tells what the senses do not tell, but not the contrary of what they see. It is above them and not contrary to them."[1]

(Take a deep breath and a sip of beverage. By now you may even need a neck massage from a loving friend.)

How Little We Know, How Much We Believe

I was driving west on I-40 between Knoxville and Nashville when I came upon a wall of fog hanging across the road. My senses told me the road came to a dead stop, but this data, as read by my senses and communicated to my mind, did not tell the whole story. Beyond the fog, the road continued. I just could not see it. If I had judged the situation by the physical evidence alone, I would have come to the conclusion that I-40 came to an end right there. And so, while our senses are usually reliable, this example reminds us that we cannot judge everything simply by the empirical method. Scientific data must be *interpreted* if we are to know what is real and what is true.

The fact is, most of what we think we *know*, we really *believe*. And most of what we have come to know has been guided by the presuppositional beliefs that make up the foundation of our worldview.

Honest Questions or Willful Disbelief?

Have you ever noticed that some people really seem to be on a quest for the truth about God, while others ridicule the very notion that truth about God might exist? I am the pastor of The Village Chapel in Nashville, Tennessee. We have been studying the life and teachings of Jesus as recorded in the New Testament Book of Matthew. Within those pages we have taken special note of how Jesus responded to people's questions about who He was, about truth, and about God in general. Jesus seemed to have had quite a bit of patience for people who had honest questions, but He showed disdain for those who were willful disbelievers.

That is an interesting distinction for the Son of God to draw. There are those people who have real, honest questions and are actually looking for answers. Their doubt is no less real than that of the willful unbelievers, but honest doubters are inclined to search for and actually hope to arrive at some answers.

A Rational Faith

While the Christian faith is rational, it cannot be reduced to rationalism. If it could, it would not be faith but just another philosophy. We would be our own gods if everything were within reach of human reason. As philosopher Mortimer J. Adler has said:

> My chief reason for choosing Christianity was because the mysteries were incomprehensible. What's the point of revelation if we could figure it out ourselves? If it were wholly comprehensible, then it would be just another philosophy. [2]

And that is the point. The Christian worldview contains both verities and mysteries—things we can know for sure, and things that simply leave us standing in wide-eyed wonder. Real life is that way, too, and this is one of the reasons why I believe Christianity to be true. I accept as a first principle that we cannot know or fully understand everything about God. The finite cannot fully grasp the infinite. But since God has chosen to reveal some truth to us through the writings of the Bible and through the life of Christ, we are not without hope. We can believe the truths of God's revelation to be true.

But the good news is that if we want to get to the truth about religion, we do not have to close our eyes to reality. We *can* and *should* keep our eyes wide open the entire time we discuss religious truths. We do not have to check our brains at the door when we begin to look into the truth about God and the Bible.

Admittedly, the church has not always maintained this attitude. In the early part of the third century, when the church was still quite young, there was quite a little stir between some key leaders. Tertullian (c. 160–225) posed the question: "What has Jerusalem to do with Athens? The Academy with the Church?" arguing that those who had become believers should not study philosophy, which would only serve to lead them into all kinds of heresy. He taught that once a person had come to belief, the revelation of God in Christ and the Scriptures was all they needed.

Clement (c. 150–215), on the other hand, believed that God had used philosophy to prepare the Greeks for the knowledge that later came through the revelation of Christ. He saw this as parallel to the way God had used the Old Testament to prepare the Jews for the coming of Christ.

As the church grew in its understanding of the relationship between divine revelation and human reason, along came Augustine (c. 354–430), who showed that the task of Christian thinking is to ascertain what is true and make good use of it. Augustine searched for a balance. He encouraged Christians to take what is good from philosophy and leave behind that which is bad. Augustine struck a balance and taught that we could be discerning thinkers and embrace all truth as God's truth.

You may have heard the story of the four rabbis who had a series of theological arguments, and three of the men were always in accord against the fourth. One day the odd rabbi out, after the usual "three to one, majority rules" statement that signified he had lost again, decided to appeal to a higher authority.

"Oh, God!" he cried. "I know in my heart that I am right and they are wrong! Please give me a sign to prove it to them!"

It was a beautiful, sunny day, but as soon as the rabbi finished his prayer, a storm cloud moved across the sky above the four. It rumbled once and dissolved.

"A sign from God! See, I'm right, I knew it!"

But the other three disagreed, pointing out that storm clouds form on hot days.

So the rabbi prayed again: "Oh, God, I need a bigger sign to show that I am right and they are wrong. So please, God, send a bigger sign!"

This time four storm clouds appeared, rushed toward each other to form one big cloud, and a bolt of lightning slammed into a tree on a nearby hill.

"I told you I was right!" cried the rabbi. But alas, his friends insisted that nothing had happened that could not be explained by natural causes.

Now the rabbi was getting ready to ask for a bigger sign, but just as he said, "Oh God…" the sky turned pitch-black, the earth shook, and a deep, booming voice echoed out, "HE…IS… RIGHT!"

The rabbi put his hands on his hips, turned to the other three, and said, "Well?"

"So," shrugged one of the other rabbis, "now it's three to two."

Like the three overconfident rabbis, some people are just dead set against reasonable discussion on issues of faith. They are not honest doubters; they are willful disbelievers. No matter how much evidence is presented or how much reason is marshaled, they will always choose not to believe.

In the end, belief does not exclude all doubt, but it does transcend it. The ultimate question is this: Do we have the courage to believe the truths we can grasp and to trust God to be in control of those we cannot?

- *Does God exist?*
- *There are many different ideas about God. If God does exist, how do we know which God is the true one?*
- *What do atheists and agnostics believe about God?*
- *Is belief in God rational or irrational?*
- *Why doesn't God just show Himself to us?*
- *What is the evidence for God's existence?*

5

How Do We Know That God Exists?

Men can always be blind to a thing so long as it is big enough.

G.K. CHESTERTON

I grew up in a climate where faith existed but was seldom questioned. After all, when you are a kid, adults tell you that Santa Claus, the Easter bunny, the tooth fairy, and God are all real. You are also told that believing in them will get you gifts, baskets of candy, coins under your pillow, and an all-powerful Someone who can help you out of any jam. So what kid would not become a believer?

As I grew older, I eventually discovered that three of the four were not *really* real. (I hope I am not bursting anyone's bubble here.) But what was I to do with the fourth? No one could show me God. So I began to ask questions like, "Does God really exist, or is He something that we made up, like a fairy tale, to help us get through life?" and "If God exists, what is He really like?"

Differing Views of God

I am not alone in this. People have been debating the reality of God for centuries. Their conclusions vary a good bit and have been influenced by a wide number of factors. Even a casual study of human history would show that there have always been some people who believed in God and some who did not. But just in terms of sheer numbers, the vast majority of people down through the centuries have held some kind of belief in a God or god(s). This belief is generally called *theism,* of which there are three different varieties.

Monotheism, which includes Christianity, Judaism, and Islam, is the belief that there is just one God who is the Creator and Sustainer of everything that exists. Monotheists believe that this God is all-powerful and all-knowing, the only self-existent being. They believe that God is not confined by time and space as we humans are. God has an intellect, a will, and a purpose behind all that He does and allows.

Polytheism is the term which characterizes most religions outside of the three monotheistic faiths. Polytheists include the ancient Greeks and Romans, as well as most Eastern religions and Native American tribes. They believe there are many different gods and that none of them are ultimately supreme. Sometimes the gods even stand at odds with one another and battle against each other. The various gods are usually defined by their job description (i.e., the goddess of love, the god of fertility, the god of the sun, the god of the moon, the god of the harvest, etc.).

Pantheism is the term which characterizes the idea that the universe as a whole is god. Here, god is not so much a personality as a force or energy which permeates the entire universe. The universe is, in a sense, god's body. Instead of having a will and an intellect, the god of pantheism is like the battery on which the universe runs. Pantheism thrives in Eastern belief systems such as Hinduism and Buddhism, as well as in the modern New Age movement.

There is a popular notion that all religions point to the same God. I wish I could say that was true, but the fact remains that they do not. At the same time, as a Christian, I do not have to believe that other religions have everything all wrong. But where they disagree, I find I am forced to make a choice.

The most obvious difference between polytheists and monotheists is in their conception of how many god-figures exist. Polytheism suffers from a difficulty in language and logic. If by definition *God* is the term that describes a *supreme* being, then God could not be limited by a job description or in any other way. As for pantheism, if god is impersonal, there is no divine viewpoint from which to determine right and wrong thinking. Therefore, how could we ever get to any "right" thinking about God? As C.S. Lewis pointed out in his book *Mere Christianity,* pantheists do not believe in a God "who takes sides, who loves love and hates hatred, who wants us to behave in one way and not in another." And so, from the pantheistic view, we have no basis for moral judgment or justice. Monotheists, on the other hand, believe that God has set specific parameters for right and wrong thinking and behavior. We are not left to guesswork. These parameters have been spelled out for us through divine revelation.

Within the major monotheistic belief systems of Christianity, Islam, and Judaism, there are also some basic disagreements. The most significant of these relates to the central figure of the Christian faith, Jesus Christ. There is disagreement about His mission on earth and whether or not He rose from the dead after being crucified on the cross. While Jews and Muslims acknowledge the historicity of Jesus Christ, and even go so far as to recognize Him as a teacher and prophet, they do not accept the reality of His resurrection or the idea that His death on the cross paid the price for our sins.

Christians, on the other hand, believe that while Jesus Christ did serve in the roles of teacher and prophet, He was really much more than that. Christians believe that Jesus was God-the-Son come to earth in the flesh with the purpose of restoring the relationship between God and humanity by dying for the sins of His people.

So, while the three major monotheistic belief systems do have some things in common, when it comes to the atoning work of Christ on the cross as the means of salvation, they are not pointing in the same direction at all.

These differences do not mean that people from these groups should go about hating each other or treating each other badly. As a matter of fact, such behavior goes directly against what most of them believe. But while tolerance is good, we should not make the mistake of equating tolerance with intellectual acquiescence by ignoring the distinctive truth claims in the different belief systems. The paths are not all the same, and we show disrespect to their beliefs if we suggest they are.

Atheism and Agnosticism

Atheists deny God's existence altogether. True atheists believe that the material world is all there is, and any reality beyond the physical realm is denied. The sense of a greater meaning and purpose to life is not part of an atheist's belief system. You live, you die, and that is all there is. German writer Jean Paul Richter (1763–1825) said of atheists, "No one is so much alone in the universe as a denier of God. With an orphaned heart, which has lost the greatest of fathers, he stands mourning by the immeasurable corpse of the universe."

Atheists do not believe the evidence for God is conclusive, and some even believe that there is evidence against the existence of God. Yet they are not able to offer any reasonable answers to the big questions of where we come from or why there is such intricate order and beauty in the universe. Because any reference to the immaterial world is out-of-bounds for true atheists, also out-of-bounds (if they are going to remain consistent) are immaterial things like love, hope, soul, and morality.

Lastly, there are those who call themselves ***agnostics.*** They claim that the human mind can never know whether or not there is a God, an ultimate cause, or anything beyond the material world. For the agnostic, such knowledge is viewed as beyond the reach of our feeble minds. The French historian Joseph Ernest Renan (1823–1892) once said that if an agnostic were to pray, the prayer would go something like this: "O God, if there is a God, save my soul, if I have a soul."

Since we are finite creatures struggling to understand the infinite, it is normal and even logical for us to have some unresolved questions about God. God would not be God if we could know all there is to know about Him. But that does not give us the right to become spiritual ostriches, burying our heads in the sand and shutting out the possibility of any knowledge of God. Curiosity about God and an innate longing to connect with Him will drive the honest seeker to want to know more about Him.

As humans, we are relational creatures. When we are alone, in the quiet of our hearts, we find that our soul's deepest hunger is spiritual and relational. We long for a connection with our Creator. This hunger could never be satisfied if God were unknowable or if He is only some sort of impersonal force that permeates the universe.

Philip Yancey once wrote that God is not "a misty vapor but an actual Person. A Person as unique and distinctive and colorful as any person I know. God has deep emotions; He feels delight and frustration and anger." This is the God of the Bible, the God who is really there, the God who wants to be known.

Some people complain that though God exists, He seems to be hiding Himself from us, as if He did not want to be found or bothered. On the contrary, as Blaise Pascal said, "Instead of complaining that God has hidden Himself, you should give Him thanks for having revealed so much of Himself."[1]

So what is the evidence for the existence of God? How do we know that God exists? In what ways has God revealed Himself?

The Evidence of God

Many things point to the existence of God. But we must bear in mind that we cannot *see* God in the same way that we see the moon in the night sky. Because God is Spirit, seeing God will require that we see with the eyes of our minds, our hearts, and our souls.

You and I believe in a lot of things that we cannot see, hear, smell, taste, or touch. We believe in feelings like love and desire, motivations like willpower and hope, forces like gravity and magnetism, even historical figures like Darwin and Nietzsche. We believe thousands of things about science, history, philosophy, and religion for which we have no immediate empirical access or proof. So what do we do?

We gather evidence, make use of our reason, and come to rational conclusions. More often than not, however, we rely on testimonies of "experts" to believe in things which lie beyond our five senses. A testimony is a witness or report presented by those who have "been there," like astronauts, molecular biologists, philosophers, theologians, or the authors of great books from previous centuries. Sometimes a testimony may come from physical evidence, such as archaeological artifacts, geological surveys, or cosmological data.

For instance, I believe that the United States of America went through a civil war in the mid-1800s, even though I was not actually there to see it happen. I might not believe in the Civil War if there were only one clue, like a single sword found in a field near Gettysburg. But the cumulative evidence convinces me: hundreds of swords, cannonballs, rifles, uniforms, letters of soldiers, books, etc. There is a mountain of evidence available that supports the existence of the Civil War, so I conclude by way of rational probability that there was one.

Likewise, I may not be able to see God with my eyes or touch Him with my hands, but there is not just a mountain of evidence—there is an entire universe of evidence that supports God's existence.

The Testimony of Curiosity

Perhaps the best place to start our search for evidence of the existence of God is where we are at right now, asking questions like these. The fact that we have a brain which can think thoughts and ask questions is what we might call the *testimony of curiosity*, our longing to know God.

Where does this interest come from? What is the source of our longing for God? Why are we so curious about something we cannot experience physically? If we have such a strong curiosity about the spiritual realm, it must at least suggest that there is a spiritual realm for us to be curious about.

When we get away from the noise and racket of our own busyness, perhaps while standing at the seashore and listening to the rhythm of the majestic ocean, or gazing up into a clear night sky salted with millions of stars, we suddenly become aware that there is something other, something larger than ourselves, something beyond what we can experience through our physical senses. And we are drawn to it by a strange combination of wonder, fear, and awe.

This curiosity also becomes apparent when we are watching something as simple as a spider spinning her web. Which way will she throw her sticky silver strand next? How does she know how to build such a well-engineered edifice? Our curiosity is aroused and we wonder, Who equipped her to perform this task? Who taught her how to do these things? And how is her web so beautiful and so well-designed?

As magnificent as the ocean is, it is not the thing we long for. Otherwise, we could live near the coast and never feel this longing again. As incredible as the heavens are, they are not what we long for either. We can see a million nighttime skies and watch a thousand science-fiction movies, imagining ourselves traveling around the galaxies at warp speed, and still not experience conclusive satisfaction. The same can be said for watching the spider, the beaver, the eagle, or the owl. In the end, they are all just road signs. They point us in the right direction, but they are not our destination.

Can this curiosity ever be satisfied? Is there anything in this world that will fulfill the longing in our hearts for that something other, that something larger and beyond what we can experience with our senses? Or does this insatiable curiosity and longing suggest we should be looking somewhere else? As C.S. Lewis has said, "If I find in myself a desire which no experience in this world can satisfy, the most probable explanation is that I was made for another world." And that is what the Christian faith teaches—that you and I are more than impersonal matter, and we are standing on the outside of a glass door looking in, longing to be reunited with the Source of our being: the infinite, personal God who alone can give our lives meaning.

For the atheist Sartre there was no infinite reference point, and so for him, life had no meaning. It was despairingly absurd. But for those who have come to believe in the God who is there, there is indeed an infinite reference point. And the good news is that this infinite reference point is not just a force or a fog, but a face. The Christian faith teaches that God has personality. It asserts that God is intelligent, can communicate, and can love and be loved. Only a God with personality can satisfy the deep-seated, spiritual longing in our souls to find our source in the universe.

And so the pull of curiosity provides us with a clue about the existence of God. It is as if God has written curiosity into our software that we would hunger to know Him and that we would never be satisfied with cheap substitutes. Sartre was right in this much: We are finite, and no other finite thing can provide us with meaning for our existence—not success, not leisure, not pleasure. Only God has the capacity to fill our lives and give our lives meaning. If we follow the road signs, they eventually point us not to a "where" or a "what," but to a "who."

The Testimony of Awareness

Another evidence of God's existence is what we might call the *testimony of awareness.* This evidence focuses on the human abilities of perceiving and processing information.

One of the things we tend to take for granted is the amazing way our five senses perceive information: the taste of lemon, chocolate, ketchup, or mustard; the sight of rich colors in a sunset on a Florida gulf beach; the smell of hot chocolate-chip cookies in one of those walk-up places at the mall; the feel of mud squishing between our toes; or the familiar sound of a dog barking at a pesky squirrel. Did our ability to perceive all these things come about by accident or by design?

Each of us has about 26 million olfactory nerve receptors per square inch in our nasal cavities. When smell particles enter our noses, they stimulate a sequence of these receptors, which in turn send a message to the lobe of the brain that mediates our sense of smell. As we go through life, our brains have stored the memory of thousands of such sequences. That is how we distinguish between the smell of hot raisin bread and our grandmother's perfume.

This same amazing complexity can be seen in our sense of taste, touch, hearing, and sight. How many different kinds of food can we distinguish by taste, such as peanut butter, pineapple, and pizza? How many voices on the other end of the phone can we identify after hearing them say just one syllable of our name? How many colors, shapes, sizes, and distances can we distinguish with our eyes? What about our ability to feel the difference between something that is smooth or coarse, hot or cold, sharp or dull? The complex systems of our five senses and the way they interact with the brain (which is far more advanced than most computers) is amazing evidence of intelligent design.

Not only are the systems themselves incredible evidence of God, but the fact that He created us with these systems tells us that He desires for us to know things. Why else would God have designed us to be industrial-strength, information-gathering, mental vacuum cleaners, able to suck up vast amounts of knowledge about the world around us? God wants us to know about Him. More importantly, He wants us to know Him.

Belief in God has been called "blind faith" by some critics of faith. But with such clear evidence as that found in the intelligent design of our five sensory systems, doesn't it take more blind faith to attribute these systems to some accidental arrangement of atoms in an impersonal universe than it would to believe they came off the design table of an intelligent Creator?

The testimony of awareness, our ability to perceive and process information, speaks of God's existence, His intelligence, and His intention for us to be able to come to knowledge about the real world we live in.

But let's look further; there is more.

The Testimony of Nature

Not only are we curious about the supernatural and capable of perceiving and processing information about the natural realm through our five senses, but we also have the testimonial evidence of the very real things that exist in the observable universe around us. The *testimony of nature* is another evidence of God's existence.

The psalmist tells us that "the heavens are telling of the glory of God" (Psalm 19:1). Have you ever tried to count the stars in a night sky? Dr. David Block, professor of astronomy and applied mathematics at the Witwatersrand University in Johannesburg, South Africa, says, "If we were to count all the stars in the Milky Way at a rate of one per second, the process would take two thousand five hundred years!" That is a lot of glory to God coming from just one galaxy.

Earth is but a tiny planet orbiting a small star, one of several billion stars in what we call the Milky Way galaxy. The Milky Way is one of 30 galaxies in what is called the "Local Group" of galaxies, which stretches some ten million light-years across.

The entire universe is estimated to be at least 15,000 million light-years across, and up to 20 billion years old. Consider again the question of origin: "Where did all this come from?" Contemplate the questions of order: "Why is the universe so beautiful and well-balanced? How could such a complex universe be so finely tuned as to allow for intelligent life on our planet?" Science answers by pointing to the laws of physics. But, as thinking people, we are compelled to ask, "Who established the laws of physics?"

In the past couple of years astronomers have become increasingly more confident about the Big Bang theory and the idea that the universe had a beginning. While the argument for God's existence is not dependent on scientific validation, it is interesting that the more science learns, the more convincing the case for the Bible's idea of God becomes. If the universe had a beginn*ing*, then it must have had a Beginn*er*, Someone who caused the Big Bang to bang.

The complexity and order of the cosmos point to an intelligent Designer, an Originator and Manager of the universe and all that it contains. Sir Isaac Newton, one of the fathers of modern science, once said, "This most beautiful system of the sun, planets and comets, could only proceed from the counsel and dominion of an intelligent and powerful Being." Nature speaks clearly and does not stutter about the existence of a Designer.

Astronomer Carl Sagan, in his SETI (Search for Extraterrestrial Intelligence) program, claimed that if we were able to find just one message with information in it from outer space, that would prove the existence of extraterrestrial intelligence. He did not claim that we would have to be able to interpret the information. We would just need to be able to identify it as *information.* That is a very interesting statement when you consider that, in the field of biology, scientists have discovered that DNA is more than just matter. It is matter that matters. A single strand of DNA "is so efficient that all the information needed to specify an organism as complex as a human being weighs less than a few thousand millionths of a gram and fits into less space than the period at the end of this sentence."[2] How is that for a microchip? DNA is so full of information, it should silence all doubt about the intelligent design evidence for the existence of God.

The Testimony of Cause and Effect

In the real world where we all live, logic tells us that every known effect has to have a cause. The fact that we exist, are aware of our existence, and can think and reason, all point to a cause. Who or what started it all and brought the very first people into existence? The *testimony of cause and effect* is another evidence for God's existence.

Some people believe that, rather than an intelligent Designer/Creator, "chance" is the cause and the answer to our questions about origin, purpose, and destiny. They suggest that the universe is the result of a big cosmic accident, and our existence and consciousness can be explained by pointing to a subsequent series of smaller time-plus-chance events, dubbed *evolutionary development.* But what is the likelihood of chance being our cause?

In an interesting book entitled *Does God Exist? The Debate Between Theists and Atheists* (Buffalo, NY: Prometheus Books, 1993), J.P. Moreland argues that Cambridge astronomer Fred Hoyle has calculated the possibilities of life arising spontaneously by chance to be similar to the probability of a tornado blowing through a junkyard and spontaneously forming a fully functional Boeing 747 out of the trash.

In his book *Not a Chance,* R.C. Sproul quotes French writer and philosopher Voltaire (1694–1778) as saying that "what we call chance can only be the unknown cause of a known effect." That is to say, chance is not really the cause of anything. When we say something happened by chance, we simply mean that we do not yet know what actually caused it to happen. Chance alone has no causal power to make anything happen because, as Sproul points out, chance is nothing. Therefore, it would be illogical to say that our existence and consciousness are a result of chance.

Indeed it is logical to assume that whatever *caused* us would have to be more intelligent and self-aware than we are because something greater cannot come from something lesser. We would naturally expect the contrast between us and our cause to be quite distinct. So distinct, in fact, that we probably would not have the ability to understand even a small bit of who He is—unless, of course, He were to take the initiative and reveal Himself to us. And at that point, we are really talking about the Christian God, not just a cosmic force.

So, who programmed you with a curiosity and longing for something beyond what this world can offer? Who designed the hundreds of thousands of nerve endings that connect your eyeball to your brain and enable you to read this book? Where did the "information-processing chip" for the million-million plus cells in your brain come from? Our hunger for the spiritual, our amazing capacity to perceive and process information, the magnificent artwork of nature, all of these serve as testimonies to the existence of God. But there are more testimonies....

The Testimony of Conscience

If you peer into a microscope for the rest of your life I doubt you will be able to find an explanation for that part of human nature which serves as the voice of moral law. The *testimony of conscience* is yet another evidence of the existence of God.

As a species, humans have a built-in sense of right and wrong, of *should* and *should not*, of *ought* and *ought not*. Yes, there are mild variations within the different cultures and civilizations down through the ages, but these variations really do not amount to much. Murder, lying, stealing, unfaithfulness, hate, and abuse of all kinds—these are activities universally acknowledged to be morally wrong. Meanwhile, charity, generosity, respecting other people, kindness, and honesty are universally seen as good. You do not have to be a philosophical genius to see that there is a difference between the actions of Mother Teresa and Adolf Hitler.

Where does this sense of right and wrong come from? It has not shown up in our blood, our DNA, or our bones. Even if it does someday, who put it there to start with? Conscience is not a simple animal instinct that we are compelled to obey, like some wild dog protecting its turf.

Some people have tried to dismiss this inner moral law by saying that moral truth is relative: "What's right for you is what's right for you, and what's right for me is what's right for me." But the logical outcome of this kind of thinking is moral anarchy. Any culture based on it is surely on its way to collapse because we humans can be such a selfish lot. What if I wake up one morning and decide that what is right for me today is that I come over to your house and steal your computer, take your wife, or paint your house fluorescent pink? Moral relativism just will not work when it comes to living in a society of more than one.

Doesn't it seem likely that the same Designer who placed Orion's belt in the sky has blessed us with a sense of right and wrong which gives balance to our existence together on earth? Instead of creating us as preprogrammed robots that could do only good, God reveals His moral law as something we can understand as well as be responsible to. We have the choice of obedience or disobedience, which we must make on a moment-by-moment basis.

At times we have all tried to avoid or deny the moral law, especially when obeying it will cost us something. Other times we are quick to appeal to it, usually when it is convenient or beneficial to us. In arguments with other people, we often depend on moral law when we protest, "That's not fair!" In order to claim that something is "not fair," we have to first acknowledge the existence of a universal way to measure fairness. Once we acknowledge that, we are back at moral law. The existence of this universal moral law points us toward God. We simply cannot have something like moral law without a moral lawgiver.

But unlike the physical laws of our universe which are compulsory (you can only ignore the law of gravity at your own peril), the moral law is optional. We cannot continue to live without breathing air, but we can and will both obey and disobey our consciences daily. With moral law we manage the health and welfare of our souls, for the good or for the bad, by the choices we make. Each and every time we make a bad moral choice, we harden our hearts. Soon we are no longer tender to the voice of our conscience.

In *Works of Love,* philosopher and theologian Søren Kierkegaard wrote of the conscience as our *connector* to God:

> A man could not have anything upon his conscience if God did not exist, for the relationship between the individual and God, the God-relationship, *is* the conscience, and that is why it is so terrible to have even the least thing upon one's conscience, because one is immediately conscious of the infinite weight of God.

Cumulative Evidence

These are only a few of the arguments that point to the existence of God. Of course, none of these arguments by itself proves the existence of God. But together these arguments serve as clues that all point to God's existence. Just as in the case of the historicity of the Civil War and almost everything else we have come to believe, it is the weight of the cumulative evidence that leads us to a logical conclusion that something is real.

I would also like to add that the existence of God is not dependent on whether you or I believe. If God does exist, He exists whether we believe it or not. And if God exists, He exists not "however you understand Him to be," but as He is in reality. If God is the very Source of all real things, then God must be more real than anything else. Our inability to comprehend very much about God is not proof that He does not exist. Rather, it is proof that He exists and goes far beyond our limited concept of reality.

The Testimony of My Life

Lastly, I will share with you from my own experience. I came to believe in God at a young age, and then later went through a time of questioning. Partly as a result of becoming disenchanted with the church, and partly as a result of an honest hunger to know what was true about God, I began reexamining the basics of Christian faith. At times, belief in God and the act of going to church struck me as a Pollyannaish "leap of faith" because it seemed like a lot of people around me had accepted the Christian faith blindly. Instead of coming to an intelligent decision about something that was objectively true, faith seemed more like a default setting for anyone born into our culture. You believe in God, you go to church. But there I was with questions I knew science could not answer, and I was not sure if religion or philosophy could either. Somehow I clung to the notion that beneath it all there was a truth that could stand the test of my honest questions.

Setting aside the stylistic and cultural differences I had with the church, I began a search for the truth. I started reading books that would help me find the places where faith and reason intersect. Great thinkers like Aristotle, who talked about how there is much more to reality than science could explain, referred to these issues (the realities that lay beyond the physical sciences) as *meta*-physical. Augustine asserted that our souls would be restless until they found their rest in God. Pascal wrote about a God-shaped vacuum inside each of us, a void that only God could fill. These and numbers of other great thinkers helped me come to the conclusion that we are not alone in an impersonal universe, and we are not the random result of a cosmic accident.

Because the real meaning of life goes beyond what can be analyzed under a microscope or programmed onto a computer chip, explaining the *how* of life just was not enough for me. I longed to know the *why* of life. Real meaning in life is more than amusement, more than self-expression, more than defining, systematizing, and reorganizing all the data we could ever collect. Such things will never answer the cry of our souls because we all are looking for something way beyond ourselves. I believe that something is a Someone.

Christianity teaches that the infinite, personal God has clearly revealed Himself. The testimonies of curiosity, awareness, nature, cause and effect, and conscience offer a *general* revelation of God. The Christian faith offers *specific* revelation of God from two sources: the written word of the Bible and the living word of Jesus Christ. They both shed light on the nature of God.

Through the Bible we can know about God. But more importantly, we discover that we can also actually *know* God. Jesus Christ, God the Son, entered time and history to make a way for us to have a relationship with our Creator. He came to invite us to become members of an invisible kingdom, a spiritual kingdom, one that is not limited to the physical realm. It is through Christ that we can find real significance in life. It is through Him that we are offered God's forgiveness and mercy, and it is by His love that we can find our way back home to our Father's house.

- *The world is full of books about religion. What is so unique about the Bible?*
- *How does a book as old as the Bible relate to us today?*
- *Isn't the Bible full of contradictions?*
- *In a nutshell, what is the Bible really all about?*
- *Who wrote the Bible and when was it written?*
- *Why are there so many translations of the Bible?*
- *Why do I have so much trouble understanding the Bible?*

6

How Do We Know the Bible Is God's Word?

All the wisdom of this world is but a tiny raft upon which we must set sail when we leave this earth. If only there was a firmer foundation upon which to sail, perhaps some divine word.

SOCRATES

Yearbooks

The other day I happened upon my old high-school yearbook. (I know what you are thinking, but do not worry. I will not be launching into a melodramatic retelling of my good ol' glory days.) As I leafed through its pages, I was struck by the fact that something as simple as a yearbook could evoke such vivid memories. There were photos of events like football games, homecoming, the prom, and graduation day. There were snapshot reminders of relationships with my best buddies, of girls I wished I had had the guts to ask out but never did, and of teachers who poured their hearts out trying to get me to pay attention long enough to learn the difference between a noun and a verb. There were tokens and mementos of clubs and cliques, athletics and academics. The yearbook was an overview of the people, places, and events that sum up those four years I spent at Falls Church High School in northern Virginia.

In a much more significant way, the Bible is a similar kind of book. It tells us about the people, places, and events that have been a part of the human drama for centuries. While it does not contain any photographs, the Bible does paint fairly detailed portraits of real men and women from all walks of life and how they related to each other and to God.

But unlike most high-school yearbooks that end up filled with those sappy, unrealistic "you're really sweet, cute, and nice...don't ever change" inscriptions, the Bible tells us the honest truth about ourselves. It speaks about how we have all gone our own selfish ways and how much we need the grace and forgiveness of God in our lives. And when the Bible calls for us to change, it even tells us how that change can take place—that God Himself will be the One to change us if we are just willing.

Most importantly, as we read the pages of the Bible, it tells us about God. It reveals who God is, what God is like, what He wants from us, and how we can come to know Him. It is a love story about God's relentless pursuit of those who would yield their lives to Him.

The Criticism

Of course, the Bible has its detractors, but isn't it ironic that many of the people who denounce the Bible most passionately have never actually read it? On what are they basing their criticism? Other people struggle with the idea that the Bible is the source of divine revelation. While many of these people would say they believe in God, what kind of God do they believe in? Is their God mute? Is He unable to speak? Is their God not intelligent enough to employ at least some basic communication skills to convey a message to them?

One thing the Bible demonstrates very clearly is that God is not mute. The God of the Bible has spoken. He has employed several means to communicate with humanity: direct verbal communication, carvings on stone tablets, the words of prophets and priests, angelic messengers, and thundering clouds. The God of the Bible is so intent on being heard that one time He even opened the mouth of a donkey to get the attention of a thickheaded prophet. And after trying for years to get a hearing from humanity via these means, God finally decided to leave the comforts of heaven, put on some human skin, and come to speak directly with as many as would hear Him. Perhaps the communication problem is not from God's side of things!

Isn't this what it all comes down to: If God were to speak, would we be willing to hear? If we believe that God is really there, that He created the heavens and the earth and is the Designer of the human eye, the Juggler of stars, and the Painter of sunsets, why on earth would we think God could not speak? If God can draft DNA, why would He not be able to inspire some of His people to write down what He wanted us to know? Believing the Bible is not nearly so preposterous as believing that God exists but is somehow unable or unwilling to communicate with us.

So let's ask the basic questions: What *is* the Bible? When was it written and by whom? How can such an ancient book be relevant to us today?

The Details

The Bible is a compilation of 66 books, divided into two major sections: the Old Testament and the New Testament. The word *testament* is another word for a promise, a pledge, or a covenant, and both parts of the Bible detail the covenants God has made with His people.

The writings of the Bible were composed over a period of approximately 1400 years (roughly 1300 B.C. to A.D. 100) and were originally written in three different languages—Hebrew, Aramaic (a hybrid language similar to Hebrew and spoken throughout the Near East from around 300 B.C. to A.D. 650), and ancient Greek. The writers of the various books came from every kind of socio-economic background, including peasants, prophets, kings, fishermen, doctors, poets, accountants, and statesmen. They included royalty and common folk, rich and poor, educated and uneducated alike. Perhaps that is one of the reasons why so many millions of people have been able to find something in the Bible that relates to their own situation in life.

The Amazing Unity of the Bible

I don't know if you have ever noticed how hard it is to order pizza when you are with a group of people, even if they are people you know well and get along with. The larger the group, the more difficult the process becomes. Two people like veggie only, two like the butcher shop's variety of meats. Three people want thick crust, one wants thin, another wants extra-extra-extra cheese. Getting even ten people to agree on what kind of pizza to order can be downright impossible.

That is also the way it can be with thoughts and ideas about religion. There are even more ideas about God, faith, and spirituality than there are topping combinations for pizza. Finding any agreement on what is true about God and what He has communicated to us can seem impossible. But this demonstrates one of the unique truths about the Bible. It was not written by some sort of mountain-dwelling, navel-gazing guru who ate hallucinogenic mushrooms one night and had a wild dream about what God is like. Instead it was written by a diverse group of individuals who represent a broad cross section of humanity. And God did not override the identities of the people He inspired to write these books. The personality of each writer comes through loud and clear, each exhibiting a unique style.

In short, the Bible does not reflect just one person's experience with the God of the universe. It is the result of God inspiring over 40 different individuals to write down the things He wanted us to know. And in spite of its wide variety of authors and their diverse backgrounds, there is an amazing harmony and unity in the Bible. The unified message of the Bible is the story of God's plan of redemption. Each author and every book paints some part of the mural. It is as if 40 different people got inspired one night and could actually order pizza together!

The Uniqueness of the Bible

The Bible is a truly unique book. No other book in history has been translated into more languages or distributed more widely around the world. World leaders invoke its wisdom, philosophers praise its truth, and countless millions have benefited from the hope and comfort found in its pages. The Bible contains a message that rings true in the hearts of hungry souls.

Down through the centuries the Bible has inspired such notables as Isaac Newton, who declared the Scriptures to be the most exalted philosophy. George Washington, the first president of the United States, said, "It is impossible to govern the world without God and the Bible." Philosopher Immanuel Kant wrote that "a single line in the Bible has consoled me more than all the books I have ever read." And Theodore Roosevelt once said, "A thorough knowledge of the Bible is worth more than a college education."

Yet in spite of all it has to offer, for many people the Bible remains unopened, unapproachable, and nothing more than a graduation gift or a place to record the family tree. Why is this so? There may be several answers, but like any other book, the Bible must be read before it can be fully appreciated.

The Relevance

As you read through the Bible, you will soon discover that its message is timeless. Although people back in Bible times did not drive cars, talk on cellular phones, or surf the Web, they did share in common a lot of the same human experiences you and I have today. They wrestled with real-life problems such as broken relationships, greed, doubt, fear, depression, anger, disease, and financial troubles. Just like us, they had a deep-seated need for significance and security. They wanted to love and be loved by God, their friends, and their families. The common characteristic we share with them is that none of us can face those problems successfully on our own. We all need God's help.

The Honest Truth About Ourselves

One of the benefits we get from reading the Bible is that it provides an honest look at ourselves. All the characters of the Bible are presented candidly and honestly, just as they really were. Even the great King David, a central and heroic figure in the Old Testament referred to as "a man after God's own heart," is shown as someone who was tempted to lust, did not have the moral strength to resist, and acted on his lust by committing adultery with another man's wife. He then sent the woman's husband off to the front lines of a fierce battle, thus ensuring this man's death so he could take the man's wife as his own. In the writing of the Bible, there was no political spin machine enlisted to make us think David had not sinned. We are shown what he did, told that it was wrong, and even shown what the consequences of his actions were (see 2 Samuel chapters 11 and 12).

So one thing is very clear: You can be sure the Bible will give you an honest look at the human condition. It reveals the good, the bad, and the ugly. And that is one of the reasons the Bible rings true for so many people; it corresponds to reality by being honest about the weaknesses of some of history's most influential figures.

The Authority of the Bible

As I noted in the quote at the beginning of this chapter, Socrates once said, "All the wisdom of this world is but a tiny raft upon which we must set sail when we leave this earth. If only there was a firmer foundation upon which to sail, perhaps some divine word." Without a doubt, Socrates had one of the sharpest minds of any person who ever lived. Yet even Socrates recognized the limitations of human wisdom. He acknowledged that in our search for real meaning in this life and hope for what happens to us in the next, we would have to find another source of truth. And Socrates knew this kind of wisdom could not and would not ever be of human origin, not ultimately authored in the mind or heart of any man or woman. It would have to come from a source higher than humanity and be what he called a "divine word."

That is precisely what the Bible claims to be: a divine word, the Word of God. That is why it has earned such a place of authority in the lives of so many people. Through the ministry of the Holy Spirit, the Word of God becomes a lamp unto our feet and a light unto our path. It illuminates the ground beneath our feet (as a metaphor for our current situation in life), and it also illuminates the path ahead to give us direction for the future.

The Questions

Socrates liked to stir people up. He was known to ask his students some pretty tough questions to challenge them in their thinking. It was his hope that they would discover truth without him having to spoon-feed it to them.

Among all the known species, we human beings are unique in our intelligence and in our capacity to think and reason. Not many cockroaches, camels, or codfish seem concerned with questions about the origin of the universe, the meaning of life, or thoughts about the existence of God. This does not mean that other species are without intelligence or skills. We see amazing engineering skills when we watch a spider spin her web, and we may learn something about aerodynamics by studying the flight of an eagle. However, no other creature ponders subjects like truth, meaning, morality, and destiny. These issues are simply beyond mere animal instinct.

Down through the centuries, philosophers and religious thinkers have dealt with "the big questions" in a variety of ways. There have been those who, believing in the power of human reason, have argued that mankind would someday be able to come up with satisfying answers to any question that might be posed. But so far that has not happened.

Other thinkers have denied the importance of these questions. They have set the questions aside, declaring that since we can never really know about these things, any attempt to do so would be vain speculation and a waste of our time. But both of these ways of dealing with our questions leave out another viable possibility.

Recognizing the limitations of human reason and conceding that there are many things beyond the reach of our intelligence, many people have acknowledged the necessity of looking outside ourselves for answers to these ultimate questions. One of the greatest minds of the seventeenth century, mathematician and philosopher Blaise Pascal, concluded, "Reason's last step is the recognition that there are an infinite number of things which are beyond it. It is merely feeble if it does not go as far as to realize that."

Let's face it. In spite of all our incredible scientific, technological, and philosophical accomplishments, human reason simply has not been able to offer satisfying answers to these ultimate questions of life. If we are to find the answers to our deepest questions, we will need to search outside ourselves. So where should we turn?

The Revelation

John Henry Newman once said, "As prayer is the voice of man to God, so revelation is the voice of God to man." *Revelation* is a term derived from the Latin *revelare,* meaning "to unveil." Revelation provides knowledge that is otherwise unavailable to us, knowledge that we could not access by thinking harder or investigating more. Revelation offers us knowledge that is simply beyond our reach, beyond human discovery. Through revelation, information is disclosed to us by an outside, more informed source.

Let me try to express this another way. While the Bible deals with revelation on a divine-to-human level, a simple human-to-human example of revelation would be a parent who tells a young child that the moon's light is not its own, but that it is a reflection of the sun's light. The child could not have figured this truth out for himself. It is simply beyond the child's reach. But as they grow, children learn many new things from the credible "revelations" of their moms and dads, older brothers and sisters, friends, or teachers. Even though all the subtle nuances of every answer may not be fully understood, these revelations are the truth made available in a simple enough form to be understood. So it is with God's revelation to us. In the pages of the Bible, He tells us truths that we could not discover for ourselves.

The Means

Just because the Bible (or any other source) *claims* to offer divine revelation does not mean that it does. Since we are reasoning creatures, we cannot blindly accept just any revelation that claims to be of divine origin without testing its veracity. This raises a question. If God were to reveal things about Himself to us, what means would He use to do it? How would the messages be conveyed?

It seems to me that true divine revelation would need to have at least three characteristics. First, it would have to be offered in an intelligible language that humans could understand, write down, study, analyze, translate, and preserve for other people to consider. If it were God's intention to communicate to as many people as possible, it seems unlikely He would offer revelation in a secret language that could only be understood by a spiritually gifted prophet or an elite few. Rather, God would likely choose a commonly used language. Such is the case with the Bible.

Second, divine revelation would be informative. It would contain propositional truth about God, mankind, morality, and the universe. Its statements would give these subjects definition and show how they relate to each other. And while information about the infinite God can never be exhaustive, that does not mean it cannot be accurate. What is revealed would be specific and applicable to real, everyday life. Such is the case with the Bible.

Third, whenever divine revelation speaks about issues we already know something about (for example, science or history), it would be relatively accurate to what we have come to know. When the Bible speaks historically, we should not find historical evidence that clearly and conclusively contradicts what the Bible says. When the Bible speaks about science, it should not contradict what has been proven beyond a shadow of doubt by scientific research. Also, when the Bible makes statements about human beings and their nature, those statements should generally hold up to what we can see in the mirror or in people on the street. For example, if the Bible were to claim that humans can live underwater or that trees can talk (not in a poetic sense, but literally), it would be fair to discount the Bible as a source of revelation. Divine revelation should be true to the realities which have been conclusively confirmed. Once again, such is the case with the Bible.

Finally, while a credible source of divine revelation might unveil knowledge that is *beyond* reason, it must not contradict the fundamentals of sound reason, otherwise we would not be able to come to a firm belief regarding the truth it claims. The law of non-contradiction, the law of cause and effect, and the basic reliability of sense perception should still be in play. Christianity is rational, but it is not mere rationalism. It is reasonable, but it does not depend solely on human reason.

I find it quite satisfying that the Christian faith has both verities and mysteries in it, that it is full of things we can verify by reason, and it contains other things that leave us standing in wide-eyed wonder. Reason gives us confidence; revelation gives us hope. The Bible speaks to us with both.

The Accuracy of the Bible

Some people have questioned the credibility of the Bible because of its age and the number of times it has been translated. But the Bible (and specifically the New Testament) is perhaps the most credible of ancient texts in existence. The New Testament was completed almost entirely within the first century A.D., close to the time Christ walked the earth, and was written by people who either knew Jesus personally or were close to someone who did.

All 27 books of the New Testament were written between A.D. 45 and A.D. 90. Someone may complain saying, "That's a pretty long time between when Jesus lived and when these things were written. How can we possibly believe the New Testament record is accurate? As many times as it was copied and recopied, it would surely have lost some of its accuracy, wouldn't it?" These are fair questions, so let's take a moment to judge the credibility of the New Testament the same way we would any other ancient text.

I think there are three things which are important to consider: 1. When was the ancient text originally written? 2. How many manuscript copies exist? and 3. How big a gap is there between when the original text was written and the dates of the earliest surviving manuscript copies?

For instance, scholars tell us that Homer's *Iliad* was originally written around 900 B.C. There are 643 manuscript copies in existence, the earliest being dated at 400 B.C. That is a 500-year gap. Or take Caesar's *Gallic Wars*, written 58–50 B.C., with only ten manuscript copies in existence, and the earliest copy dated at A.D. 900. That is almost a 1000-year gap. Even worse, how about Plato's *Tetralogies*, dated 427–347 B.C. There are only seven manuscripts in existence, with the earliest copy dated at A.D. 900. That is a 1200-year gap.

So how does the New Testament compare to these other ancient texts? As I mentioned above, all 27 books of the New Testament were completed by the end of the first century A.D. There are 5366 manuscripts or partial manuscripts of the New Testament in existence, and the earliest manuscript copies have been dated to within 100 years of their original composition. That is less than a 100-year gap![1]

If you judge the New Testament the same way you do other ancient texts, the New Testament is clearly the most trustworthy of all ancient documents. In the writings of the New Testament, we have a very credible source of historical data.

The Contradictions?

One of the most common criticisms aimed at the Bible is this: "Isn't the Bible full of contradictions?" Now, *full* is a pretty strong word. It gives the image of a book with blatant contradictions on every page and in every paragraph. Once again, this complaint is usually put forward by people who have never actually read the Bible. If asked to point out one of these contradictions, they usually shrug their shoulders and confess that they do not have any specific examples.

Of course there are difficulties in translation and interpretation, but these are not about issues which, even if proved true, would disprove the overall message of the Bible. We would be foolish to discount the Bible based on a few insignificant trivialities.

There are certainly things in the Bible that could be classified as *paradox*—something which appears to be a contradiction but may very well be true. But a paradox is not a contradiction. Most apparent contradictions in the Bible are pretty easily resolved by taking a look at some additional historical or cultural information. Others can be resolved by allowing for literary genre, such as when the writer/speaker employs parable, metaphor, or poetry. Another thing that is often mistaken as a contradiction is *mystery*, and the Bible contains some incredible mysteries. A mystery can be defined as something unexplainable but not inconceivable. Truths made known by divine revelation and believed through faith would certainly qualify as mysteries.

The Translations

I am often asked, "Why are there so many different translations of the Bible?" Granted, there are quite a few. But clearly the Bible itself is not the reason for this. The simple fact is that the English language is quite fluid and is continually evolving. Words come to have different meanings with each cultural shift. Because of this fact, if we are to understand what the Bible writers meant at their time, in their particular cultural setting, we will constantly be adjusting our translations of the ancient texts to reflect the authors' originally intended meaning. (If you have had difficulty reading the Bible because of some language barrier, let me encourage you to look around for another translation. There are many available, and there is sure to be one that will speak in terms you can understand. Most Christian booksellers will be able to offer you helpful advice in picking one out.)

So What Is in the Bible?

In the end, it is the content of the Bible that provides us with the most convincing proof of its truthfulness and authority. I have often used the acronym EATEA (pronounced ee-tee) to describe how the Bible unveils divine knowledge in these fundamental categories of thought: epistemology, anthropology, theology, ethics, and aesthetics.

The Bible Speaks About Epistemology

> The fear of the LORD is the beginning of knowledge; fools despise wisdom and instruction (Proverbs 1:7).

Epistemology is the study of the nature, sources, and limits of knowledge. It seeks to answer the questions of what we can know and how it can be known. There are many opinions about precisely what we can know and with how much certainty we can know it. But somewhere, after all the arguments have been heard, we all have to put our intellectual feet down on something as a starting place.

The Bible distinguishes between the wisdom of this world (1 Corinthians 2:4-6) and the wisdom of God (1 Corinthians 2:7-14). The wisdom of this world is limited to what man can know on his own without the help of God through revelation. It is limited to knowledge we can obtain through our five senses. If someone holds to a belief that God does not exist and that the natural world is all there is, then obviously, matters of spirituality will not make sense to that person.

The Bible teaches that human nature includes a spiritual component, and that our five senses are ineffective in comprehending the spiritual realm (1 Corinthians 2:14). Through reading and hearing the truth of the Bible, the Spirit of God brings faith to our hearts by revealing the mysteries of God to us and offering insights into who we are as spiritual and moral creatures.

The Bible acknowledges that humans are intelligent (Isaiah 1:18), but that real knowing begins with a fear and respect of God, the Author of knowledge (Proverbs 1:7). Wisdom, the ability to efficiently employ knowledge, is also to be found in the fear and respect of God (Proverbs 9:10). The Bible claims to be God's timeless word to mankind (Isaiah 40:8; Mark 13:31). As such, it offers us access to an incredible wealth of knowledge (2 Timothy 3:16-17). The Bible is indeed a divine word, illuminating all of life, offering hope for the future and providing that "firmer foundation on which to sail" for which Socrates longed.

But as gatekeepers of our own minds, we must recognize that the wisdom of the Bible is not preprogrammed into us. We have to take the time to read it ourselves and to meditate on it, becoming ever more familiar with the truth it contains. The Bible is a means of grace, the hearing of which gives rise to faith in our hearts. As we search the depths of Scripture, a practical working knowledge of the things of God is revealed to us by the Spirit of God.

The Bible Speaks About Anthropology

> God created man in His own image, in the image of God He created him; male and female He created them. God blessed them; and God said to them, "Be fruitful and multiply, and fill the earth, and subdue it; and rule over the fish of the sea and over the birds of the sky and over every living thing that moves on the earth" (Genesis 1:27-28).

Anthropology is the study of the human person. From the Bible's pages we find helpful information about our origin, purpose, and destiny, as well as honest information about our nature and character.

First, the Bible speaks about our origin—that we were lovingly and carefully designed by God (Psalm 139:13-16). This stands in contrast to the atheistic, antisupernatural view, which suggests we are the result of an accidental arrangement of chemicals. The Bible's view leads us to hope. The other view ultimately leads us to despair.

Second, the Bible speaks about our purpose. It tells us that among all things created, humans are the only part of creation that was made *imago dei*, in God's image and likeness. On that basis, we may deduce that human beings were created to reflect the image of God. Since God is infinite, every finite human life has value, dignity, and purpose because each of us can reflect God's image. You might say humanity is like a giant disco mirror ball, each of us one of the small mirror panels reflecting some small part of the infinite God.

In the Bible's view, our destiny is to be restored to our function as image-bearers of God by coming to know Him personally, loving Him fully, and living with Him forever. The Bible also teaches that each of us will remain a unique individual personality throughout eternity. This stands in contrast to other religions that view God as an impersonal force and each human a part of that force, destined upon death to be assimilated into the impersonal, cosmic unity.

The Bible Speaks About Theology

In the beginning God...(Genesis 1: 1).

Theology is the study of God, His nature, and His relationship with mankind. Without the revelation of the Bible, we would know very little about God, and what we could know would be vague at best. But the Bible offers an answer to the question, "Does God exist?" by pointing out that before anything else existed, God already was, and that He created everything *ex nihilo*, or out of nothing (Genesis 1:1).

In answer to the question, "What is God like?" the Bible gives us many insights into His character: God is love (1 John 4:8); God will one day be our Judge (Romans 2: 5); God is forgiving to those who confess their sin and repent (1 John 1:9); God knows everything (Psalm 139:1-6); God is supreme and almighty (1 Chronicles

29:11). And above all, the Bible reveals that God is personal and wants us to know Him.

The Bible also documents God's actions in history. This does not mean the Bible documents *all* of God's actions on this planet or elsewhere in the universe. But we are given exactly the information God wants us to know (Revelation 22:18-19). That is to say, as God inspired the writing and directed the compilation of the Bible, He did it with intention, purpose, and design. The information in the Bible was not accidentally discovered by us, nor was it accidentally revealed (2 Timothy 3:14-17). God is behind both the revealing and the understanding of His Word.

The Bible is a book about restoring the relationship between an almighty God and the creatures He created (1 Corinthians 1:21). It is about a relationship between a loving Father and His often wayward children (Galatians 4:4-6). It talks about our rebellion and God's forgiveness, how in spite of our self-centeredness, there is a way we can have peace with God through Christ. It is about the God who is there and His eternal plan for humanity.

The Bible Speaks About Ethics

> For such is the will of God that by doing right you may silence the ignorance of foolish men (1 Peter 2:15).

Ethics is the set of moral principles and values by which we determine right and wrong. Everyone has a general sense of the moral law. Everyone understands that there are some things that are "right" and some that are "wrong" in life. We have all found ourselves saying, "Hey, that's unfair!" If there is such a thing as "fair," then there has to be some standard, a moral law by which we can judge what is fair and what is unfair. Where did this law come from? Since it is propositional, not biological, moral law must have an intelligence behind it. Then who is the moral lawgiver?

The Bible teaches that there is a nonhuman, nonrelative basis and source of universal moral law. Contemporary theologian John Stott has said,

> Christians cannot go along with secularists when they agitate for unlimited permissiveness in social and ethical terms, nor when they foolishly imagine that "free thought" is intellectual freedom or that "free sex" is moral freedom. For Christians are convinced that neither truth nor righteousness is relative, since God has given us (by revelation) absolute standards both of what is true and of what is right.[2]

We live in an era when there is great confusion about issues of public and private morality, and many people now believe that moral values are relative or "up to the individual." This confusion arises in part from the fact that we are a pluralistic society. There is disagreement on which set of values should serve as the norm for all of society.

The only remedy for a culture or an individual is to recognize that we need an outside source, one that offers clarity on what is right and what is wrong, a source that we can use like a compass to help us find our way.

The Bible Speaks About Aesthetics

> For since the creation of the world His invisible attributes, His eternal power and divine nature, have been clearly seen, being understood through what has been made, so that they are without excuse (Romans 1:20).

Aesthetics is the branch of philosophy which deals with the nature and appreciation of beauty and art. The Bible tells us that throughout the created universe we see evidence of God's creativity and His penchant for beauty. In Genesis, the Bible says that after God created the elements of the physical universe, there was no form, and that all was in chaos. Then God began to design and arrange, to bring order and form to the cosmos. He created light, land, vegetation, and all living things. The Book of Genesis tells us that God stopped and assessed His work and saw that it was "good."

In the Scriptures, beauty has a purpose. It points like a road sign to the Author of beauty. The significance of the beauty of nature declares God's glory, reminding us of God's majesty, power, authority, and generosity. God did not have to make anything, as He was not lacking in any way. He did not need to make humanity because He was lonely or needed someone to talk to. God simply chose to create as an expression of His own creativity and was generous enough to give humanity the ability to appreciate all He has made. That is why we stand in silent awe beside the mighty ocean, dumbfounded at the foot of the majestic mountains, or drawn heavenward under a star-filled sky. There is unmatched beauty all around us, and all of creation cries, "Glory to God!"

God Has Spoken

God's divine revelation in the Bible speaks to both the heart and the mind. If the Bible only spoke to the heart, it would leave us open to all sorts of romantic delusions. If it only spoke to the mind, it would leave us with a lifeless and hollow intellectualism. How wise of God to intentionally reach out to us in this holistic way.

In Psalm 32:8-9, God spoke through King David and said this:

> I will instruct you and teach you in the way which you should go; I will counsel you with My eye upon you. Do not be as the horse or as the mule which have no understanding, whose trappings include bit and bridle to hold them in check, otherwise they will not come near to you.

God's guidance does not come under compulsion as in the way we guide a horse or mule through the use of bit and bridle. Rather, He will guide us with instruction and counsel so that we can employ the God-given gifts of intelligence, reason, understanding, and free will. He will use His Word, the Bible, to teach us about Himself, about how we can know Him, and how we should conduct our lives on earth with each other. But God does not force this information on us. We will have to open the book and read it, meditate on it, ponder what it says, and pray for insight to learn what it means. When you read the Bible, use the eyes of both your mind and your heart. Pray for the Holy Spirit to teach you. Ask God to show you what you need to see, and then ask Him for the courage and will to respond to what He shows you to do.

- *How can we learn more about spirituality and spiritual growth?*
- *Can the Bible help in this area?*
- *How should we interpret the Bible?*
- *Are we supposed to take everything in the Bible literally?*
- *How should we apply the message of the Bible in our lives?*

7

Learning: How Do I Interpret and Apply the Message of the Bible?

The [written] Word is the wire along which the voice of God will certainly come to you if the heart is hushed and the attention fixed.

F.B. Meyer, *The Secret of Guidance*

Not long ago, I received a forwarded e-mail from a friend who knows how much I enjoy dealing with questions. The content of the message (whose original source is unknown) was a list of simple, sometimes humorous questions that cause you to think about how often we miss the rather obvious. Here are a few examples:

- Why isn't *phonetic* spelled the way it sounds?
- Why are there interstate highways in Hawaii?
- If a cow laughed, would milk come out her nose?
- If you are in a vehicle going the speed of light, what happens when you turn on the headlights?
- You know how most packages say "Open Here"? What is the protocol if the package says "Open Somewhere Else"?
- Why do we drive on parkways and park on driveways?
- Why is it that when you transport something by car, it is called a shipment, but when you transport something by ship, it is called cargo?

Some things in life are obvious. Some things become obvious after you give them just a little thought. When it comes to spirituality, if there is one thing that has become more and more obvious to me, it is that spiritual growth doesn't happen automatically. You do not just lie back and say, "Okay, God. I've accepted Christ as my Savior. Now, You do Your thing. Hit me with holiness!" and then *ZAP!*—all of a sudden, you are a more godly person, you have a more effective prayer life, and you run around always singing songs from the latest praise-and-worship CD.

In the context of Christian spirituality, we come into a relationship with God by grace alone through faith alone. This means that all the hard work has been done by God. We simply respond to the free gift God has offered us by placing our trust in Christ. Our salvation cannot be achieved. It must simply be received. But this is just the starting point of the Christian life. Then we begin the process of following Christ and nurturing spiritual growth in our everyday lives, and it is this part that requires more active participation from us.

Nurturing Spiritual Growth

Spiritual growth is fostered in the same way my wife goes about working in the garden in our backyard. Every spring, she begins to weed, seed, and feed, and then stands back and watches as God brings about the growth. It might appear on the surface that Kim is doing most of the work, but when you think about what it takes to create and manage a universe containing just the right kind of solar system, with just the right kind of planet, with just the right kind of complex ecosystems, to provide an environment suitable for plant life, not to mention human life...well, you probably get the point. Both God and Kim are involved in the overall goal of growing a healthy garden in our backyard. God provides all the power; Kim helps to nurture the growth. This is similar to the way it is for us as we pursue the goal of growing spiritually.

Spiritual growth (what theologians call *sanctification*) requires a partnership between God and us, a kind of *concurrence.* In no way does this idea negate our total dependence on God's grace. We do not "score points" with God because we are involved in our spiritual growth. God already loves us beyond measure. But if we are to grow, it does require effort on our part. As Dallas Willard has said, "Grace is not opposed to effort, it is opposed to earning." Our job is to weed, seed, and feed, but it is God who causes the growth. Concurrence reflects what the apostle Paul meant when he urged believers to "work out your salvation with fear and trembling," realizing that it is "God who is at work in you, both to will and to work for His good pleasure" (Philippians 2:12-13).

How do we weed, seed, and feed ourselves spiritually? What do these metaphors represent in practical terms?

Just as weeding a garden involves removing undesirable things that are growing in it, spiritual weeding might be confessing our sins and turning away from undesirable words, thoughts, or deeds in our lives. This requires repentance and experiencing God's forgiveness.

Seeding a garden means planting those seeds we want to grow into healthy plants. In our spiritual lives this might be sowing the seeds of God's Word in our hearts and minds; that is, learning through reading, meditating on, and coming to a fuller understanding of what God has said through the Bible.

Feeding a garden includes watering and fertilizing. Spiritually, this might be nurturing our growth through the spiritual disciplines of worship, prayer, fasting, solitude, giving, and service.

In this chapter, I want to focus on seeding: learning from God's Word. Learning leads to growth. The apostle Paul told us that "faith comes by hearing, and hearing by the word of God" (Romans 10:17 NKJV). The Bible makes it clear that God really does want us to know Him and also to know something about Him. As we study the Scriptures, God's Spirit speaks to our minds and hearts, leading us deeper into our relationship with Him. Spiritual learning results in deeper knowledge, belief, and understanding. It involves the mind, the will, and the heart.

Faith Seeking Understanding

If you are like many people, you have probably had an experience where you opened the Bible at random, read a few verses in some book like Leviticus, and then determined you did not have a clue what in the world the Bible was all about (especially since you do not own a one-year-old she-goat, and even if you did, you are not too sure you would have the stomach to sacrifice it on the church altar as a burnt offering).

The fact is, for most people the Bible can sometimes be hard to understand. Interpreting what the Bible actually says and applying it to contemporary life can also be difficult. When trying to interpret what the Bible says, we are looking for its *meaning.* When trying to apply what the Bible says to our lives, we are looking for its *significance.*

I was following a car the other day that had a bumper sticker on it that read: "Give Me Ambiguity or Give Me Something Else." It reminded me of how some people prefer that spirituality remain separated from reason and logic, limiting their spiritual life to only the mystical, experiential, and undefinable. But why should we compartmentalize spirituality off into the irrational and subjective side of life, leaving our minds completely out of the picture? God gave us minds. Doesn't He expect us to use them?

Anselm of Canterbury, who lived from about 1033-1109, thought so. He defined *theology* as "faith seeking understanding," and this begins to clarify what is so exciting about Christian spirituality. It calls for a full integration of faith into all of the rest of life and suggests that you do not have to leave your mind behind when it comes to spirituality.

When a lawyer of the Pharisees approached Jesus and asked Him, "'Teacher, which is the greatest commandment in the Law?' Jesus replied: 'Love the Lord your God with all your heart and with all your soul and with all your *mind.*' This is the first and greatest commandment" (Matthew 22:36-38, emphasis added NIV). Jesus was quoting from the Hebrew Shema found in Deuteronomy 6:5, but interestingly, the Shema only mentions loving the Lord with all your heart, your soul, and your *might.* For the lawyer of the Pharisees, a person who made his living with his mind, Jesus changed *might* to *mind.* (Since the Scriptures are God's Word, the Son of God had a right to do that.)

When we step back and look at the complete picture, we see that the combined message of the Old and New Testaments is that we are to love God with all that we are, with all that we have, with all that we do—in essence, with every faculty of our being.

Loving God with our mind happens when we spend time reading the Bible, meditating on its timeless truths, and prayerfully considering how God might want us to apply those truths to our life.

Approaching the Bible

I cannot tell you how many times I have opened the Bible and begun to read without giving the least bit of thought to what I was doing. It is like that old joke about playing Bible roulette: A guy is desperate for guidance from God, so he cries out, "Lord, speak to me!" He throws open his Bible and randomly reads the first verse his eyes fall on, which says, "And he went out and hanged himself."

Not satisfied with that, the fellow closes the Bible, riffles through the pages again, reiterates his prayer, "Lord, please speak to me!" and opens the Bible back up. This time it says, "Go thou and do likewise."

Obviously, this isn't a great way to approach reading the Bible, especially if you are looking for its true meaning and significance. God gave us brains and expects us to use them, including when we are reading His Word. So how should we approach reading the Bible?

The apostle John recorded something Jesus said that has helped me with my approach toward reading the Bible. In John 16:13, Jesus tells us that the Holy Spirit will guide us into all the truth. Here is that idea of concurrence again. Once I have taken the time to read the Word and humbly pray, asking the Holy Spirit to guide me into the truth, Jesus has promised that the Spirit will lead me to something that will help me grow spiritually.

Sometimes it is truth for my mind. Sometimes it is encouragement for my soul. Other times it is a warning about some temptation with which I may be struggling.

The point is, we need to approach the reading of God's Word alert and with anticipation. So before you even open your Bible, ask yourself this: "Am I approaching the Bible expecting to hear from God?" As F.B. Meyer has said, "The [written] Word is the wire along which the voice of God will certainly come to you if the heart is hushed and the attention fixed."[1]

This is the kind of thing Jesus was referring to when He would say, "He who has ears to hear, let him hear." We all have two sets of ears: those on the sides of our head and those in our heart. If the ears of your heart are inclined toward God when you approach the Bible, you are in a much better condition to hear the voice of the Holy Spirit as He leads you into a greater understanding of God and His truth.

Another important element in our approach to reading God's Word is having a teachable disposition. The question to ask ourselves is this: Do we truly desire to know what God thinks about a specific subject, even if it runs against what we would prefer to hear? Or are we simply looking for God to agree with the position we hold? One of my favorite Bible teachers, John Stott, expressed it this way:

> If we come to Scripture with our minds made up, expecting to hear from it only an echo of our own thoughts and never the thunderclap of God's, then indeed he will not speak to us and we shall only be confirmed in our own prejudices. We must allow the Word of God to confront us, to disturb our security, to undermine our complacency and to overthrow our patterns of thought and behavior.[2]

Interpreting the Bible

Once we have our hearts turned toward heaven in our approach to reading the Bible, how do we go about interpreting what we read in the pages of Scripture? Do we have to have a seminary degree to understand it? People will say, "Well, that's your interpretation. Everyone is entitled to their own interpretation." But does their attitude justify reading almost anything we want into what the Bible says? Should we completely disregard the idea that each of the original authors had something specific in mind as he wrote?

The Clarity of God's Word

The Westminster Confession makes it plain that the Bible is clear enough in all its central teachings for anyone to understand.[3] That does not mean there are not some difficult passages. It just means the most important ideas are conveyed in a clear, easy-to-understand way. It also does not mean we will not benefit from listening to trained Bible teachers and theologians. It just means that the basics of what God wants us to know are accessible to anyone who approaches the Bible with a hungry heart and an open mind. The only requirement is that we open the book and actually read what it says.

The apostle Paul, who wrote two-thirds of the New Testament, summed it up this way as he was writing to his young protégé Timothy:

> Continue in what you have learned and have become convinced of, because you know those from whom you learned it, and how from infancy you have known the holy Scriptures, which are able to make you wise for salvation through faith in Christ Jesus. All Scripture is God-breathed and is useful for teaching, rebuking, correcting and training in righteousness, so that the man of God may be thoroughly equipped for every good work (2 Timothy 3:14-17 NIV).

Notice again these phrases: "from infancy you have known," "able to make you wise for salvation," "useful for teaching, rebuking, correcting and training in righteousness," "so that the man of God may be thoroughly equipped for every good work."

Paul would not say that about a book whose meaning was either unclear or completely up for grabs. On the contrary, Paul's view of Scripture was that it had been clear to Timothy when he was much younger, and now that he was a young adult, the Scriptures would be clear enough to help him with spiritual and moral clarity and correction.

The Power of God's Word

Long before the apostle Paul wrote those words, God spoke through the Old Testament prophet Isaiah and declared, "So is my word that goes out from my mouth: It will not return to me empty, but will accomplish what I desire and achieve the purpose for which I sent it" (Isaiah 55:11 NIV).

Did you catch that? God intends for His Word to accomplish something and to achieve something. Some of the literary images of the Bible clarify what God intends His Word to accomplish and achieve. In the vivid poetry of Psalm 119, the psalmist says, "Your word is a lamp to my feet and a light to my path" (verse 105). How might we interpret what this is saying? The metaphors "lamp" and "light" clearly refer to something that will illuminate what would otherwise be dark. The metaphor "my feet" could refer to where I am standing right now, my immediate life situation. "My path" could refer to the future just ahead or around the corner.

Sometimes the path we walk in life can be dark and uncertain, but into that darkness comes the light of God's Word to brighten where we stand now and to cast light in the direction we should turn next. The Word of God helps us evaluate the present, to see if what we are currently doing is in His will. It helps us discern the wisdom of God for our future steps in life, enabling us to make wise choices that will preserve our integrity and bring glory and honor to Him.

Handling the Scriptures Accurately

There are many good ideas about how to get the most out of a passage. Above all, we must keep in mind that we are dealing with the Word of God, which was written down in space-time history, but has eternal significance. Therefore, interpreting and applying the Bible is really more like an art than a science. As Paul wrote to Timothy, "Be diligent to present yourself approved to God as a workman who does not need to be ashamed, *accurately handling* the word of truth" (2 Timothy 2:15, emphasis added). How can we make sure we are handling the Bible accurately?

The answer to that question can get a bit involved, and it might seem to read like the directions for assembling a riding lawn mower. But if you have a large cup of coffee going and can hang in there with me for a few paragraphs, I would like to give you some tips I have found helpful in my own study of God's Word.

1. ***Read through the entire passage casually.*** Try to get the overall gist of what is being said. Take note of who the key players are, what action takes place, and especially how God, Jesus, or the Holy Spirit are involved.

2. ***Identify the literary genre of the passage.*** This is critical for accurately interpreting the passage. The Bible is rich in literary styles, and before you can accurately interpret what a passage is saying, you should identify what kind of literature you are reading. You should not interpret or apply the poetry of the Psalms the same way you would the direct statements found in the Ten Commandments. Some of the literary genres found in the Bible are:

- *Historical narrative*—Some people have suggested as much as three-quarters of Scripture is historical narrative. This genre gives us the historical account of the relationship between God and humankind and can be found throughout the Old Testament books such as Genesis, Exodus, and Judges. In the New Testament, books such as Luke and Acts are rich in historical narrative. This kind of literature describes actual historical events, such as when God made His covenant promise to Abraham, when God delivered the people of Israel out of bondage in Egypt, the struggle of Israel with its neighbor nations, the life and times of Jesus, and the birth and growth of the early Christian church.

• *Law*—The Bible is full of God's instruction for moral and ethical behavior. There is *apodictic* law, which refers to the general principles of God's law, such as those expressed in the Ten Commandments. (Webster defines *apodictic* as "expressing... necessary truth.") These laws were delivered directly by God to the people, written out on stone tablets. Then throughout the New Testament, Jesus and the apostles dealt with the application of the law to those to whom they were speaking or writing.

In the Old Testament there are also individual *case* laws, which clarified what the people of Israel were to do in very specific situations. In addition, there are *civil* laws and *ceremonial* laws, which gave the Israelites guidance in societal and religious matters.

Most Bible scholars agree that while the apodictic law remains relevant to contemporary situations, individual Old Testament case laws, civil laws, and ceremonial laws are no longer pertinent.

• *Prophecy*—There appear to be two kinds of prophecy in Scripture: *fore*telling and *forth*-telling. A prophet was doing the former when predicting what would happen in the future, and the latter when speaking on behalf of God, pointing out sin, or calling the people to some specific action. Interpreting prophecy can be difficult because it is often highly symbolic and metaphorical, and some prophecies have more than one fulfillment.

• *Poetry*—The Book of Psalms is a good example of biblical poetry. It is filled with beautiful lyrics and poetic images. Hebrew poetry bears little resemblance to much of modern poetry, which can sometimes end up being simply about coming up with words that rhyme. The Psalms are deep, honest, and direct, expressing a wide range of human experiences and emotions.

• *Wisdom literature*—The Book of Proverbs is a good example of wisdom literature. It is full of short, pithy sayings that might contrast a wise person with a foolish person or give practical instruction for life. Wisdom literature can be found throughout the Old Testament Scriptures, especially in Ecclesiastes and Job.

• *Epistles*—*Epistle* means "letter." In the New Testament certain books were actually letters written to a specific group of people dealing with a specific teaching error or moral problem. Epistles include books such as Galatians, Ephesians, and Philippians. Interpreting these books must always be done with an awareness of what was going on with those people, in those locations, at those times.

• *Parable, metaphor, hyperbole, and so on*—In His parables, Jesus used earthly stories to make heavenly points. He made up many stories in which common, everyday things like coins, sheep, weddings, and farming became metaphors, similes, and analogies to teach His listeners about the kingdom of heaven. Most parables have one main point with an occasional secondary point or two. We should avoid overinterpreting the parables by trying to assign significance to every little detail.

Jesus also used hyperbole—that is, exaggerating—for effect, as when He said, "If your right eye makes you stumble, tear it out and throw it from you." It would be a grave mistake to make a literal interpretation of this command. Jesus knows we would struggle just as much with lust having only one eye. In the context of this passage, He is pointing out that temptation not only comes from without, but also from within. Nowadays, we are not as used to hearing hyperbole as Jesus' contemporaries were, and reading a passage like this can cause some of us a great deal of anxiety (and possibly some pain!) as we try to figure out what it really means.

• *Apocalyptic literature*—There are books of the Bible that include highly symbolic imagery representing the struggle between God and the forces of evil. They include the Book of Revelation and portions of the books of Daniel, Isaiah, Ezekiel, and Zechariah. Interpreting these passages can be difficult, and there are differing views on how to do this. But the good news is that, even if you have little idea how to interpret the details of apocalyptic passages, you can rest assured that, in the end, God always wins.

Identifying the literary genre of the passage you are studying will be immensely helpful as you seek to discover what God is saying through that passage. There are other ways of classifying biblical literature, and if you desire to look into this further, I highly recommend the book *Let the Reader Understand* by Dan McCartney and Charles Clayton (Wheaton, IL: Victor Books, 1994).

3. ***Learn as much as you can about the author's historical-cultural setting.*** This can be critical to finding out what the author intended to say. We have a quite different understanding of so many things today, from social habits to spiritual disciplines to civic duties. What was it like when the writer was alive? What was his political, social, or cultural setting like? What language did he speak? Whom was he addressing when he wrote?

There are some great Bible study reference tools that can help you with historical-cultural research. You might pick up a study Bible like the NIV *Study Bible* or the *New Geneva Study Bible.* And there are a great many resources that can help you with more intensive study.[4]

(If you are still with me, you deserve to stretch, yawn, and take another sip of your favorite java!)

4. *Set the scene of the passage.* By this I mean visualizing in more detail the "who, what, when, where, and how" of the passage. Take special note of the key people and places involved. How many people were there? What were the surrounding buildings and terrain like? What action took place? What conflict or tension arose? Sometimes the richest learning comes from imagining yourself

walking around the dusty walls of Jericho in the fourth row of the Israelite marching band, or going out on the boat with the disciples on the stormy sea, or singing praise choruses while chained to a wall in a dark, damp, rat-infested prison cell with Paul. The purpose of setting the scene is not to read something into the text that is not there, but rather to support the main point of the text by bringing some details to life.

5. ***Allow what is clear to interpret what is not so clear.*** If you are having difficulty figuring out what is meant in a certain passage, look for something about that same subject from another passage of Scripture. This is often called the "analogy of Scripture" or "allowing Scripture to interpret Scripture." It is a very important tool in staying true to the message that God is trying to convey to us through His Word. For example, if you were wondering why Jesus keeps referring to Himself as the "Son of Man," you could cross-reference Daniel 7:13, where you would find out that was a title that signified the Messiah who was to come.

6. ***Distinguish between the descriptive and prescriptive passages.*** The historical Book of Acts is largely *descriptive.* It describes events—for instance, what happened when the Holy Spirit came at Pentecost to permanently live in every believer for the first time. There was an upper room, a mighty rushing wind, and "tongues as of fire," and the apostles "began to speak with other tongues." Does this mean we must be in an upper room, should expect to hear rushing wind, see tongues of fire, and begin speaking with other tongues (other languages) when we become believers and are filled with the Spirit for the first time?

Clearly this passage is not meant to be *prescriptive,* that is, establishing teaching about how the Spirit will fill every believer. It is simply descriptive of what the Holy Spirit did on one particular and unique day. On the other hand, the Book of 1 Corinthians contains mostly prescriptive material, including some direct teaching about the Holy Spirit and spiritual gifts from Paul the apostle. Prescriptive passages are much more appropriate for establishing biblical doctrine than are descriptive ones.

Applying the Message of the Bible to Everyday Life

If we are going to learn and grow spiritually, we must begin to see that reading the Scriptures is not just about knowing information. It is also about *transformation.* For that to happen, we must apply the truth of the Scriptures to our everyday lives.

This is a very sensitive thing to do, and it requires the guidance of the Holy Spirit. Without His leading, we can get into all kinds of strange thinking by mishandling the truths of the Bible. So as you begin to wonder how a given passage might apply to your own life, pray and ask the Holy Spirit to lead and guide you. Remember that the Bible as a whole is about how much God desires to be in relationship with His people and how He has gone out of His way to make this possible through what Christ did on the cross. This concept should serve as a backdrop to virtually every passage.

One of the best things we can do when looking for appropriate applications is to ask ourselves what points of identification we might have with the original writer, the subject matter, or the original recipient(s) of the writings. Was the author struggling with something we are also struggling with? Does the subject matter talk about something directly relevant to our time? Were the original recipients of the passage distracted or discouraged in a way that we can identify with? These and other questions can help answer the "So what?" of the passage you are studying. They can lead you to practical application as you find yourself identifying with Elijah's doubt, Peter's denial, or the Galatians' distraction from the message of God's grace.

The Bible and Spirituality

Christian spirituality has been compared to a journey. Once we make the initial commitment to follow Jesus, our spiritual journey has begun. Along the way, there are twists and turns, hills, thrills, and spills, blessings and blowouts. As with any journey, we must know which direction we are headed before we can make any progress.

If you live in Washington D.C., and you want to drive to Florida, which direction should you go? Could you head out in a northwesterly direction and ever make your way to Florida? I suppose you could, if you did not mind going all the way around the globe before you ever made it to Florida. But most people would not want to do that, and that is why we have things like maps. They tell us the best direction to head when we are traveling between two points. Florida is south of Washington D.C., and that is the best direction to head if you want to go there.

When we are looking for ways to grow spiritually, the Bible is the map that offers us the best information. It tells us which direction to go, what kind of terrain we must traverse, what kind of roads and highways we can expect, and some helpful information about the landmarks we will see along the way.

The Bible has been carefully prepared by God for the spiritual pilgrim who takes the time to read it and reflect on what it says. The Bible documents the interaction between God and humankind over the centuries. It shows us that we were all made with the capacity to know God, and that we will find fulfillment in our spirituality only when we are in a right relationship with God. It warns us that, as we travel on our journey, along the way we will be tempted toward distrust, distraction, and despair. It equips us with knowledge about how we can resist those temptations and what to do should we fall down or wander off the main road.

The Bible deserves to be read, interpreted, and applied with respect for its divine authority, with hope for its transforming power, and with an openness to discerning its benefits. And whatever we do with it, let's not think that merely reading and accurately interpreting the Scripture is all there is to learning. Christian spirituality is not just about filling our minds with correct spiritual data. We were not created as machines, and we were not designed to have a "virtual" spirituality. Christian spirituality is about living in a dynamic relationship with God, and studying the Bible is learning from the Word that comes from God's heart. "For the word of God is living and active and sharper than any two-edged sword, and piercing as far as the division of soul and spirit, of both joints and marrow, and able to judge the thoughts and intentions of the heart" (Hebrews 4:12).

- *The world has seen many great religious leaders, so what is so special about Jesus?*
- *Why has Jesus Christ remained such an important figure in human history?*
- *How do we know what Jesus was really like?*
- *What makes people think that Jesus was the Son of God?*
- *Why did Jesus have to die on the cross?*
- *Everybody quotes and misquotes Jesus all the time. What is the essence of His teachings?*
- *He lived so long ago. How do the teachings of Christ relate to me today?*

8

What's So Special About Jesus?

Coming to His hometown, he began teaching the people in their synagogue, and they were amazed. "Where did this man get this wisdom and these miraculous powers?" they asked.

MATTHEW 13:54 NIV

Souvenir Shops

Nashville became our hometown in the mid-1980s. During that time, the popularity of country music was on the rise. Country music celebrities knew they had made it to the big time when they could afford to open their own souvenir shops on the north end of the famed Music Row. This shopping district became known as Souvenir Row. It was a beehive of activity for fans and tourists. At any one of these shops you could buy CDs, cassettes, posters, and photo magazines of popular country music stars, as well as coffee cups, cowboy hats, T-shirts, and beach towels. Some shops even had "cars of the stars" on display. There were lots of flashing lights, free food, and karaoke music performed by sequined, would-be country stars. All this glitz was designed to pull in as many fans and tourists as possible.

If you had come for a visit, were short on time, and were still trying to figure out which was the *best* souvenir shop (you know, the one where you could find that special Elvis Hair Shampoo and Conditioner you had been looking for), it could get confusing.

Which shop should you go to? More than one had a sign that boasted "The Biggest Selection!" or "Best Souvenir Shop in Nashville!" As the shopaholic's lament goes, "So many shops, so little time."

When it comes to religious leaders, it is a little like those Nashville souvenir shops. So many leaders have been called "special" in one way or another. And a handful of them have stood the test of time, exerting a lasting impact on succeeding generations. Some of these historic figures have led their followers to higher understandings of issues like peace, justice, social equality, and compassion for those less fortunate. Others have motivated their followers to pursue lives of self-denial, simplicity, and solitude. And still others have enlightened us by teaching with great insight about God, humanity, and the universe in which we all live.

But among all these great religious leaders, there is one who stands out from the crowd. His impact has been greater than any other religious figure in history. Oddly enough, He never made a big deal out of social or political issues. He did not appear to be concerned about image or celebrity. As a matter of fact, He often avoided crowds. He never appeared on television, never had a radio talk show, and never built a megachurch. He never went to seminary, never wore a suit and tie, and never carried a King James Bible. He never sang "Rock of Ages," "Amazing Grace," "Kum-Bah-Yah," or "Pass It On." And I would venture to say that if He had lived in Nashville in the mid-1980s, He probably would not have been the kind of celebrity that would have justified opening a souvenir shop on Music Row. His name was Jesus of Nazareth, and He was a poor Jewish carpenter who walked the planet for a little over 30 years in first-century Palestine.

The Real Jesus of History

I am aware that you probably already have an image in your mind when you read the name "Jesus Christ." Perhaps it is a nice image attached to a Sunday school workbook you drew pictures in as a child. Or maybe it is a negative image created by something you heard one of His clumsy followers say when talking to you about salvation as you sat together on an airplane. Or maybe your image of Jesus is vague and confused, scrambled by a series of hard questions that plague your heart and mind.

Whatever the case, in the next few pages I would like to invite you to take a fresh look at Jesus. Why don't you push the reset button in your heart and mind, setting aside your preconceived ideas, so you can approach the real Jesus of history without any baggage?

The first thing we need to clear up is that Jesus of Nazareth, the one called the Christ, was not a folk hero or a mythological figure like Jack in the Beanstalk or Zeus. Jesus was an actual human being, a real person, with hair, eyes, a nose, a chin, knuckles, knees, and toes. Had you lived back then, you could have touched Him on the shoulder, looked Him in the eye, and felt Him pat you on the back. You could have seen Him smile at the approach of children and heard Him speak as He taught the Sermon on the Mount.

What do we know about His life? Well, as the Christmas song tells us, He was born in the "little town of Bethlehem," a few miles south of Jerusalem. His family moved north to the Galilean town of Nazareth, where He grew up learning the trade of carpentry from His legal father, Joseph. As far as we know, Jesus worked in the family business until He was 30 years of age, most likely building tables, chairs, doors, plows, and oxen yokes for His neighbors in and around Nazareth. Given what we know about Him now, it is safe to assume that, as a carpenter, Jesus probably did some fairly creative work. I would not be surprised at all if He and Joseph had hung a sign in the window of their shop that read "Best Carpentry Shop in Nazareth."

A Case of Unlikely Celebrity

Nonetheless, before He started His public ministry, Jesus probably would not have been the first person you thought of when casting your vote for the *Jerusalem Journal's* "Man of the

Year" award. He was poor and lived in an occupied territory. During His public ministry He was disliked by the religious establishment, and at the end of His ministry even the crowds who followed Him turned against Him. Then He was hung on a Roman cross to die the death of a common criminal, convicted on a trumped-up charge brought against Him.

And yet, in the 2000 years since Jesus walked the earth, more has been written about Him than about any other figure in human history—more than Julius Caesar, King Arthur, Elvis, and John Kennedy all put together. The teachings have been studied, scrutinized, and analyzed by more people than the teachings of Aristotle, Albert Einstein, and Sigmund Freud combined. The simple truth is this: Jesus of Nazareth is the most-talked-about individual who ever lived.

A Case of Mistaken Identity

To find the real Jesus, we must look past all the popular misconceptions about who He is. It should not surprise us that someone who has been the subject of so much discussion is misrepresented from time to time. This is certainly the case with Jesus. Some people have reduced Jesus to a hippie-like guru philosopher, whose only message is peace, love, and forgiveness. Other people portray Jesus as a harsh and angry prophet bent on executing judgment and meting out punishment for even the slightest moral failure or social faux pas. Still other people have depicted Jesus as a bisexual or a homosexual, as if sexuality was the central issue by which Jesus defined Himself.

So who was the real Jesus? Was He like the common pictures of a good-looking, long-haired, West Coast "surfer dude" with deep-blue eyes, a sharp jawline, and a dark tan? Or could He be like the flannelgraph Sunday school materials portray Him: a peaceful-looking teacher, clothed in robe and sandals? In these pictures He is almost always smiling and holding a lamb or a child in His arms.

But how does that fit with the Jesus who turns over tables in the temple and then throws everyone out? And what is this about Him excoriating the religious leaders of His day for their legalism and hypocrisy? Why did He raise moral standards to such unreachable heights? Did He demand perfection from those who would follow Him?

When you compare them with the best historical accounts of Jesus, most of these modern ideas about Jesus can be seen as nothing more than fanciful, revisionist interpretations. They have little connection with the historical facts. They reveal a tendency to treat Jesus' life and teachings like you would a salad bar, picking the items you like and leaving the rest. Worse still, some people have brought their own ingredients to the salad bar and left them there, hoping other people will try Jesus *their* way.

There are a lot of people who form their concept of the real Jesus from these imaginative misrepresentations. They come to believe that Jesus was really the equivalent of the way some actor in a film has portrayed Him, the way He looks in a painting or on a poster, or the way an author arbitrarily describes Him in a book. But these ideas about Jesus are usually just the musings of irrational romantics who use Jesus like a religious action figure, dressing Him up in the costume of their choice: one time as a mysterious, transcendental guru; the next as a humanistic, super social worker; and the next as a single-issue political activist.

Where should we look to find the real Jesus? As with any pursuit of historical fact, we should search for sources which display the qualities we associate with credible historical evidence. These would be sources that will give us specific details from eyewitnesses that contain verifiable names, events, places, and dates—information that can be corroborated by outside sources that have themselves proven to be credible. From this kind of material it would be possible to get an idea of who the real Jesus of history was, what He actually did, and what He really taught.

The Biography of Christ

To use an old adage, I suggest we get it "straight from the horse's mouth." We should look at who Jesus claimed to be. The essence of His personal claims will tell us more about Him than anything else. They will reveal why He was so different and why His message to humanity was so convincing, so convicting, and so timeless.

There is one small difficulty we face in getting the "straight scoop." Jesus did not leave any writings behind. He never wrote a book Himself. But then again, neither did Socrates. Yet we have learned much about Socrates and what he said through the writings of one of his students, a man named Plato.

The writing of a good biographer can be a window into someone's life, especially if that person were an eyewitness to the key events of the story. If you were no longer around and I wanted to know something about you, but you had left no tangible record of yourself—no photos, no book, no videotape or voice recordings, I would not be left in the dark. The best thing I could do would be to look to the people who knew you and were closest to you. If they told me about you, then I would know something of what you were really like and the kinds of things you said and did. And even though some people might not have the whole story, by checking and cross-checking my sources I could still get a pretty credible account about the real you.

That is exactly what we find in reading the New Testament. It contains four personal and intimate biographies of Jesus written by eyewitnesses who were His students and friends. It is like looking at a scrapbook about Jesus' life. The first four books of the New Testament—Matthew, Mark, Luke, and John—give us a record of His birth, life, teachings, deeds, death, resurrection, and ascension.

Two of these books, Matthew and John, were written by men who were actual disciples of Jesus. That is to say, they knew Him personally. They walked Palestinian roads together, sat around campfires together, stayed up late at night telling stories and laughing until they all cried. They heard the very words of Jesus as He preached powerful sermons in synagogues, on hillsides, at the shorelines, or in the cities. They saw with their own eyes as Jesus opened the eyes of the blind and the ears of the deaf. They helped Jesus pass out the food that day He fed thousands from a little boy's lunch pail, and they witnessed other miracles from His hand.

Mark's Gospel, though actually written down by Mark, is believed to have been taken from an account verbally dictated by Peter, one of Jesus' closest disciples and friends. Through Mark, Peter gives us his version of the amazing deeds of the real Jesus of history. Peter was there in that overcrowded house on the day Jesus commanded a severely paralyzed man to take up his stretcher and walk. He was in the room when Jesus commanded a little dead girl to come back to life and watched her rise up. He was in that nearly swamped boat when Jesus commanded a violent storm to be still, and it stopped immediately. And on one unique occasion, Peter, James, and John were up on a mountaintop with Jesus when they got to peek behind the curtain of heaven as Jesus straddled the natural world and the supernatural world right before their very eyes. They got to eavesdrop as Jesus talked with none other than the Old Testament heroes Moses and Elijah.

Luke was an educated physician. With a doctor's eye for details, he tries to provide the most accurate portrait possible, telling us about the real Jesus of history. In his opening remarks he describes the arduous process of "having *investigated everything carefully* from the beginning" and then tells us the purpose of his writing, which was "so that you may *know the exact truth* about the things you have been taught." Sounds like a man who was out to discover what really happened and report with precision the facts he uncovered. Isn't it interesting that a man of science would become one of the key persons to investigate and convey the truth about the most significant religious figure in history?

Luke is believed to have written his record of the life and teachings of Christ with the help of Mary, the mother of Jesus. Knowing what my mom knows about me, I think Mary could have provided some fairly credible eyewitness accounts of the real Jesus of history. Wouldn't it have been great to hear her stories about Jesus?

The Bible tells us that Jesus was born of a virgin. That certainly makes Him unique. If that had not actually happened, then Dr. Luke or someone like him could have refuted it with some degree of credibility. He could have at least hedged his bets by simply leaving it out of his book. Instead, Luke placed it right at the beginning where it could not be missed.

Taken together, these four accounts provide an indisputably accurate and strikingly complete picture of who Jesus was and what He said about Himself.

The Claims of Christ

So what did Jesus say about Himself? A look at the personal claims of Christ as recorded in the four Gospels will reveal that they really are quite unusual. These four credible accounts record Jesus making statements like: "Believe in God, believe also in me," "I am the way, the truth and the life. No one comes to the Father except through me," "If you knew me, you would know my Father," and "Whoever has seen me has seen the Father."

And after He was arrested, when Jesus was dragged before the high priest, He was asked a point-blank question: "Are You the Christ, the Son of the Blessed One?" (*Christ* is the Greek form of the Hebrew word *Messiah,* so what the priest was really asking was: "Are you the Jewish Messiah?") How did Jesus answer that direct question? He said, "I am; and you shall see the SON OF MAN SITTING AT THE RIGHT HAND OF POWER, AND COMING WITH THE CLOUDS OF HEAVEN" (Mark 14:61-62—words in small caps are Jesus quoting Messianic prophecy from Psalm 110 and Daniel 7).

Sounds pretty incredible, doesn't it? Jesus claimed to be one with God. He claimed to be *the* way to God, not just *a* way to God. He claimed to be *the* truth, not just *a* truth; *the* life, not just *a* life. Then, to top it all off, Jesus told the Jewish high priest that yes, indeed, He was the long-awaited Jewish Messiah.

But that is not all. Throughout the four Gospels we see Jesus doing other things that no normal human being in his or her right mind would ever do. They include:

- Making statements in which He claimed that He was the fulfillment of many other significant Old Testament prophecies. Jesus claimed that the sacred, holy, ancient Jewish Scriptures actually pointed directly to Him.
- Accepting the worship of many people who fell down at His feet. He accepted what should only have been given to God.
- Forgiving people of their sins, not just sins committed against Him, but all their sins. That is an authority only God can claim.
- Saying that on judgment day He would be the One to decide the fate of all. That is definitely something only God could do.

At this point, someone may very well ask, "What are you trying to say? What does this mean?"

C.S. Lewis pointed out that anyone who made these kinds of claims would have to be one of three things: a liar, a lunatic, or the Lord Himself. To use another alliteration, the claims of Christ show Him to be either a deceiver, deluded, or the Divine One. There really is not much else you can say of someone who claims to be God. He would have to be an arrogant, out-and-out con artist; a liar of the worst kind; or a certifiable nutcase, a completely deluded megalomaniac with no concept of reality. And if any of these cases are true, then the real Jesus of history should not be taken seriously at all. Both He and His ideas ought to be locked up and silenced forever.

On the other hand, if none of those explanations fit, then we must conclude that He was who He claimed to be: the Lord Himself. And if that is the case, then Jesus and His message deserve to be taken quite seriously indeed.

In John's Gospel, Jesus is called the "Word" of God, as in the *living* Word or the Word become *flesh.* This past year, my wife and

I received a Christmas card from some friends which said it well: "The Word did not become a philosophy, a theory, or a concept to be discussed, debated, or pondered. But the Word became a person to be known, followed, enjoyed, and loved."

Jesus was a real person who did some incredible things that can only be explained if a person is willing to accept the claims He made about Himself. When Jesus claimed that He was both God and man to the Jewish religious leaders, they thought this was nothing short of blasphemy. And if Jesus had not been God in the flesh, they would have been right. But the fact remains that everything Jesus did confirmed that He was who He said He was.

Since the days Jesus walked the earth, many people have thought of Him as a great prophet or priest. Even most of the non-Christian religions of the world acknowledge Jesus Christ as a great teacher. But as we have seen, the real Jesus of history did not think of Himself that way. Neither did the writers of the New Testament. And for two centuries, the overwhelming consensus of Christian thought has been that Jesus is much more than a great teacher.

No other major religious leader or philosopher has made the kinds of claims Jesus made. Quoting C.S. Lewis again:

> There is no parallel in other religions. If you had gone to Buddha and asked him, "Are you the son of Bramah?" he would have said, "My son, you are still in the vale of illusion." If you had gone to Socrates and asked, "Are you Zeus?" he would have laughed at you. If you had gone to Mohammed and asked, "Are you Allah?" he would first have rent his clothes and then cut your head off.[1]

Jesus was truly unique. Even His mission bears that out.

The Mission of Christ

The mission of Christ was stated very clearly by the angel who came to explain to Joseph why Mary, his fiancée and still a virgin, had turned up pregnant. The angel said:

> Joseph, son of David, do not be afraid to take Mary as your wife; for the Child who has been conceived in her is of the Holy Spirit. She will bear a Son; and you shall call His name Jesus, for He will *save His people from their sins* (Matthew 1:20-21, emphasis added).

Then later on, Jesus Himself stated His mission with great clarity: "For the Son of Man has come *to seek and to save* that which was lost" (Luke 19:10, emphasis added) and "the Son of Man did not come to be served, but *to serve, and to give his life a ransom for many*" (Matthew 20:28, emphasis added). This was reiterated by the apostle Paul who said, "It is a trustworthy statement, deserving full acceptance, that *Christ Jesus came into the world to save sinners,* among whom I am foremost of all" (1 Timothy 1:15, emphasis added).

Without a doubt, the primary mission of Jesus was to come into the world to die for the sins of mankind, to save us from having to face the judgment of God on our own merits. Portrayals of Jesus as just another prophet, priest, or moral teacher simply fall short of recognizing this.

Jesus did not come just to teach us how to love each other more, although He did do that as well. Jesus did not come just to call us to become social activists, to rise up and counter the inequities of this world, although He did teach that we are to be responsible agents of God's resources and that we should share with anyone who is in need. Jesus did not come just to help us get in touch with ourselves or free our inner child, although He did say that we must have the humble faith of a child to enter His kingdom.

Jesus came for the primary and expressed purpose of voluntarily laying down His life as a sacrifice for ours, to pay the price for our sin, to purchase our salvation, and to satisfy the holiness of God. Jesus came so that by His grace, you and I may enter into an eternal relationship with the living God. If you read the New Testament, there is just no mistaking this fact.

Theologians refer to this act—Christ paying for the sins of the world—as the "Atonement." It is an act of God's grace, the giving of a gift which cannot be earned. And it is offered freely to all who believe. This is where we get to the heart of the uniqueness of Jesus Christ.

This teaching is unique among the religions in the world. Christianity promises that forgiveness and mercy are available to all who call upon the name of the Lord. It is not offered on the basis of our merit or obedience, but solely on the merit of Christ's death on the cross.

Not only do the claims of Christ and mission of Christ show Him to be unique in all of history, the message of Christ echoes His uniqueness.

The Message of Christ

What did Jesus teach and preach? Was it only about love? Was it just a feel-good message encouraging us to do random acts of kindness? Can the message of Christ be reduced to a simplistic tolerance? Let's look at what Jesus actually said.

The first passage in which we read of Jesus preaching reveals the essence of His overall message: "Repent, for the kingdom of heaven is at hand" (Matthew 4:17).

That is certainly not the recommended way to start a preaching career. The very first recorded words of Jesus break all accepted public-speaking rules. What happened to opening with a "warm the crowd up" humorous anecdote or a feel-good human interest story? But that is not Jesus' style. He begins His ministry by telling people they need to repent. He says there is something wrong with us, and we all need to be changed, shaken up, and turned around. Not exactly a page out of *How to Win Friends and Influence People*, is it?

So what does this word *repent* mean—a word that stands in such a central position, right at the beginning of the message of Jesus Christ? The Greek word used in the New Testament is *metanoia,* and it means to have a change of mind that institutes a change in life. Repentance has both a reflective and an active side.

The reflective side means recognizing that we really are sinners and coming to the place in our lives where we feel remorse for our sin. It means understanding that the reason we feel guilty for some of the things we have done is because we really *are* guilty. It is coming to the place where we stop passing the blame, stop offering God our lame excuses, and admit our faults. Each of us has broken God's laws. When we finally stop trying to deny it, we have taken the first step of repentance.

Contrary to what pop psychology teaches, guilt is not always a bad thing. Guilt is good when it tells you the truth about yourself so that you can begin to face reality and do something about it. You and I cannot find forgiveness if we live in a narcissistic fairy-land, denying that we ever do anything wrong.

Repentance also has an active side to it. True repentance is doing something about what you say you believe. We are not pre-determined or preprogrammed to do wrong by factors such as genetics, environment, or circumstances, which are out of our control. Jesus' summons to repentance speaks about human dignity, showing us we are not subject to our animalistic tendencies, and calling us to something higher than mere intellectual assent or some kind of emotional experience. It calls us not to be *hearers* of Jesus' message only but to also become *doers* of His message.

According to Jesus, repentance is a prerequisite for entrance into the kingdom of heaven. If a person will not repent, that person cannot enter the kingdom of heaven. That is drawing a line in the sand and asking us on which side of the line we will stand. If you repent, you stand with Christ. If you will not repent, you stand alone. On the reflective side, if a person will not admit his or her need, that person will not recognize his or her need for Christ. On the active side, if a person will not turn away from his or her sin, that person has not truly repented.

To put it another way, if people will not look up to God, they will miss it when God reaches down to them with the free gift of forgiveness. Repentance and forgiveness begin with humility, with bowing before the living God. We must bow intellectually, we must bow morally, and we must bow spiritually. Then by His grace, God takes care of the rest. This is the essence of the unique message of Christ.

In addition to the claims of Christ, the mission of Christ, and the message of Christ, the impact of Christ also speaks of His uniqueness in history.

The Impact of Christ

How can anyone explain the impact of this poor carpenter-turned-rabbi? How is it that the Western calendar came to turn on His life? How is it that 2000 years later artistic renditions of His face still grace the covers of major news magazines around the world? How do you explain the fact that nearly a third of the world's population identify themselves as His followers by calling themselves Christians?

Nowadays, some people think that faith should be a private affair, something they should keep to themselves. Fortunately that has not always been the case. Since the time of Christ, the contents and ideas found in His teachings have had a profound impact on millions of people who have come into contact with them. In addition to their personal impact, the fundamental truths of His teachings have provided the motivation behind significant humanitarian and social-justice efforts led by such notable personalities as William Wilberforce, Martin Luther King Jr., and Mother Teresa.

Because of his specifically Christian convictions, Wilberforce led the abolitionist movement in England to rid the world of the scourge of slavery. Because of his specifically Christian convictions, Martin Luther King Jr., founded the Southern Christian Leadership Conference and became a key figure in the civil rights movement in the United States. Because of her specifically Christian convictions, Mother Teresa of Calcutta worked among the sick and poor of India, which gained her the respect of the Nobel-prize committee and even the cynical press corps from around the world.

Wilberforce, King, Mother Teresa, and countless other people have all taken their lead from the real Jesus of history. They have followed His example in spite of the costs and inconveniences involved. They have laid down their lives for other people, as Jesus taught: "Greater love has no one than this, that one lay down his life for his friends" (John 15:13).

But make no mistake about it, Jesus also had an impact on everyday people like you and me. Many of His best friends were ragtag, uneducated fishermen. But after they met Him, their lives were transformed and they rocked the world with the message of the gospel.

When Jesus walked the earth He healed many who were sick, yet in the lives of the people Jesus healed, He was more than a physical healer. The Gospels tell the story of a man who was hiding behind a tree beside the road one afternoon. He was the picture of death: full of disease, wrapped in scrap cloth and bandages, wheezing, and coughing. When he saw the crowd coming his way, he stumbled out from behind the tree and approached the man in front, the man they called Jesus.

The crowd gasped in horror. Most shrank back to avoid contact. Some turned their heads in revulsion at the hideous man wrapped in bloody rags. Some even picked up rocks, preparing to drive the man away. But before they could, the man fell down in front of Jesus. With a raspy voice he garbled out these words: "Lord, if You are willing, You can make me clean."

At that moment, all eyes shifted to Jesus to see what He would do. And it was then that Jesus did the unthinkable. Matthew, who was there that day, tells us, "Jesus stretched out His hand and touched him" (Matthew 8:3).

The crowd was even more shocked now. Touching a leper was forbidden. Even the disciples must have cringed in horror. Why did Jesus do this? It was against Jewish law. The man was declared unclean. Why did Jesus risk contracting this horrible illness? Didn't He care about His own well-being?

There is no other disease which so isolates a person from the rest of humanity as leprosy. This man had no hope of getting better. He was just waiting for the end. His was a cold and hollow existence, void of any human affection. There was no physician on earth who could help him. But Jesus extended His hands and touched this man. One Bible commentator explains that the Greek verb translated here "to touch" was more than just a glancing touch. It is more like "the kind of grip you need when you're pulling someone up from dangling over a cliff."

This touch included something the man had not experienced in years: the full embrace of another human being. Any leper would have been thrilled to have been cleansed with just a word or by washing in some kind of miracle water, but Jesus went beyond all that. He became personally involved.

Jesus did not see just a leper. Jesus saw a man—perhaps a husband and father, someone who had not hugged his wife or held his daughter in years. How the man's heart must have ached. The decay in his body must have reflected the horrible decay eating away at his heart.

And then Jesus touched him.

I cannot wait until I get home to heaven and I can sit down and talk with that man. I will bet that day is still as vivid in his memory as if it had happened just yesterday. While it is significant that Jesus healed the man's disease, it is just as significant that He also healed the man's lonely heart. And we never forget experiences like that.

What's So Special About Jesus?

The questions about Jesus must always come down to these: What do you make of Him? Who is Jesus Christ to you? Is your soul in need of His healing touch? Just like the leprous man, all you need do is fall down at Jesus' feet, acknowledge your need, and ask for cleansing.

There has never been anyone like Jesus. Having made the claims He did about Himself, having come to die for our sins, having challenged us to see the honest truth about ourselves, and having inspired and motivated so many people to want to be like Him—only God could have done all of this.

The writer of the New Testament book entitled Hebrews said it this way:

> God, after He spoke long ago to the fathers in the prophets in many portions and in many ways, in these last days has spoken to us in His Son, whom He appointed heir of all things, through whom also He made the world. And He is the radiance of His glory and the exact representation of His nature, and upholds all things by the word of His power (Hebrews 1:1-3).

That is what's so special about Jesus.

- *What does it mean to trust God?*
- *How can we be sure God has our best interest in mind?*
- *Is God trustworthy?*
- *How can trusting God help me with my fears?*

Check Out Receipt

Monroe Library
360-794-7851
sno-isle.org

Thursday, September 5, 2019 4:37:22 PM

Title: Henry David Thoreau : a life
Due: 09/26/2019

Title: Letters and papers from prison
Due: 09/26/2019

Title: Answering the big questions about God
Due: 09/26/2019

Total items: 3

You just saved $87.98 by using your library.
That is the suggested retail price of the
item(s) checked out.

Check It Out! A podcast for lifelong learners.

http://sno-isle.org/podcast

9

Trusting: How Can I Learn to Trust God More?

In God, we live every commonplace as well as the most exalted moment of our being. To trust in Him when no need is pressing, when things seem going right of themselves, may be harder than when things seem to be going wrong.

George MacDonald

I like to drive. No, let me rephrase that. I like to be the one doing the driving.

There. I admitted it. I am a control freak. Trusting other people just does not come easy to me.

One of the reasons I was drawn to my wife is because she has what I call an SRF (strong right foot). By that I mean she does not hesitate to use the skinny pedal on the right when she is driving. She does not speed and she is not at all reckless, but she does drive with determination, and when navigating traffic calls for decisiveness, she can rise to the challenge.

However, in spite of my appreciation for Kim's driving acumen, I still have difficulty turning over the wheel to her. When we are going somewhere and she is the one driving, I say dumb things like, "You might want to turn on your lights. It's getting dark." For some reason I do not think she'll notice that the big fireball in the sky is going down, the moon is coming up, and the streetlights are flickering on.

Then, after she pulls out of the driveway, there are other things I feel compelled to remind her about: traffic patterns, directions, use of blinker, following too close, speed limits, getting in the right lane to exit, and lots of other strategic driving moves I would make if I were the one behind the wheel.

Understandably, all of this is quite annoying to her, and eventually she makes me aware of it by offering to pull off the road and turn over the keys. She is not being snippy. She is right. I need to let go. I need to trust her with the driving. I need to be reminded of my obsession with control.

Trusting others does not come easy for me, even when the person I should be trusting is trustworthy, even when the task is small. For some reason, it is hard for me to trust someone else to be in charge.

Trusting God can also be very difficult for me. It is not that I doubt God's ability. I know that if God can create and manage the entire universe, He must be capable of handling the problems in my little life. I am just not sure about His resolve to manage things *my* way.

Leaving the Driving to Him

At times God seems unpredictable, and I cannot figure out precisely what He is up to, which way He is leading me, or why. I pray, and then pray some more, hoping to gain some clarity. But sometimes, even when my world seems to be falling apart, heaven appears to be running silent. Isn't God listening? Doesn't God care?

Has that ever happened to you? If so, do not worry, you are not alone. There are many of us. We may have varying levels of anxiety and different things we like to control, but the problem is still the same. We basically have difficulty trusting God because it means we have to let go of the steering wheel and leave the driving to Him.

How should we handle our hesitancy and inability to trust God? That question reminds me of a day in the life of Jesus' disciples that is recorded for us in the fourth chapter of Mark's Gospel:

> On that day, when evening came, He [Jesus] said to them [the disciples], "Let us go over to the other side." Leaving the crowd, they took Him along with them in the boat, just as He was; and other boats were with Him. And there arose a fierce gale of wind, and the waves were breaking over the boat so much that the boat was already filling up. Jesus Himself was in the stern, asleep on the cushion; and they woke Him and said to Him, "Teacher, do You not care that we are perishing?" And He got up and rebuked the wind and said to the sea, "Hush, be still." And the wind died down and it became perfectly calm. And He said to them, "Why are you afraid? How is it that you have no faith?" They became very much afraid and said to one another, "Who then is this, that even the wind and the sea obey Him?" (verses 35-41).

It was none other than President Franklin Roosevelt who said, "We have nothing to fear but fear itself," but I am still not sure I can agree with him. I believe in the correspondence theory of truth, which says, "Truth is that which corresponds to reality." Reality tells me that this world is a very dangerous place, and the fact is, you can get hurt out there! There are a thousand things that can happen to you. You can drown in a stormy sea, get bit by a snake, fall off a ladder, contract a rare Himalayan disease; there are any number of things that are worthy of your fear.

For you chronic worriers, if you ever run out of things to worry about, there is a book with a list of things you might not have thought of before. It is full of fears that are sure to catch your worrying eye. Called the *Paranoid's Pocket Guide* (Chronicle Books, 1997) it includes examples like these:

- One in 6500 Americans will be injured by a toilet seat during his or her lifetime.
- If you sneeze too hard, you can fracture a rib. If you try to block a sneeze, you can rupture a blood vessel in your head or neck and die.
- Nearly a third of all bottled drinking water purchased in the United States is contaminated with bacteria.

- Each year, you face a 1 in 13 chance of suffering an accident in your home serious enough to require medical attention.
- Seventeen people are electrocuted every year by hair dryers.
- Last year, nearly 16,000 cheerleaders required emergency-room treatment for injuries including sprains, torn knee ligaments, skull fractures, and even paralysis. One of the most dangerous routines, the Human Pyramid, has been banned in North Dakota and Minnesota schools.

I do not want you to become paranoid, but just think about the risk factor involved if you were a cheerleader who caught colds easily, drank bottled water, and used a hair dryer every day!

The fact is, all of us have to face some pretty scary stuff in life. Trusting God is not just an option for us; it is a necessity! But as we look a little closer at the story of Jesus and the disciples out on the stormy sea, perhaps we will see that trusting God is also a wonderful privilege, a privilege that can set us free from living a life filled with anxiety.

The Significance of Trusting in Christ

By recording the account of Jesus calming the storm, Mark wanted to remind us that when our life becomes difficult—even if we are out on a lake during a violent storm, our sails and oars useless, our boat filling up with water, our ship ready to go down—even in those stressful times, those of us who are followers of Jesus still have an option. What is that option? What can we learn from the boat trip that Jesus took with His disciples? There are three main points I see in this story.

Trusting Christ Does Not Mean We Will Always Have Smooth Sailing

Now, please do not get mad at me. I know what you are thinking, and I have thought it, too. When we first believed in God, He was in the same category as Santa Claus, the Easter bunny, and the tooth fairy. God was one of those wonderful children's fairy-tale characters whose job it was to make sure we are always safe, comfortable, and happy. How could it be God's will for us to have to go through storms?

As we grow up, we come to realize how this kind of thinking is really a trivialization of the life of faith. It is a shallow, self-centered view of who God is and the "good" He wants to bring about in our lives. The reality is, our spirituality is worked out in the real world, where life throws at us both curveballs and the stress that accompanies them. Our spiritual life is simply not compartmentalized from the other parts of real life.

We live in a fallen world, and Christians are not exempt from going through storms. We do not get to sidestep all of the stuff that sometimes makes life incomprehensible and almost unbearable. All the same bad things happen to those who place their trust in Christ that happen to everyone who does not trust Christ. Anyone who tries to tell you different is not telling you the truth. When the storm that Mark describes came up, it took the disciples completely by surprise. It was overwhelming, sudden, and shocking. They knew their lives were in danger, and they were filled with fear and anxiety.

If we use the disciples' storm as a metaphor, what could a storm represent in our lives? Storms could be pictures of those unforeseeable and unavoidable events in our lives that startle us, stun us, and knock us off balance. Just like physical storms, these events can be large and overwhelming, or small and annoying. They can be like destructive hurricanes, or like showers that drop just enough rain to get our cars dirty.

Storms might symbolize the divorce of a couple you always thought would make it, or something as small as stubbing your toe on the bathroom door. They might represent an automobile accident, or a minor argument at a family gathering. They might signify hearing your dentist say those two words we all dread: *root canal*, or having a business luncheon fall through. The metaphor touches more on the unexpected nature of these events, the way they can catch you off guard and throw you for a loop.

When most of us encounter a storm, the first thing we do is ask questions such as, "Why is this happening to me? Did I forget to pray today? Is God mad at me? Was I unkind to children or small animals yesterday?" Although these may be honest questions and may possibly be helpful at times, they really do miss the point. Storms are not always a result of sin or our lack of spiritual discipline. God is not in a spiritual slap fight with us, and the storms we encounter in life are not always some kind of punishment for the wrong things we do or the right things we fail to do. Just look at the way it happened in the lives of the disciples that day.

Whose idea was it to get into the boat in the first place? Who said, "Let us go over to the other side"? That's right, it was Jesus' idea. What were the disciples doing when the storm hit? They were in the boat taking Jesus to the other side. They were in the right place, doing the right thing at the right time. They understood what Jesus wanted them to be doing and where Jesus wanted them to go, and they were following His lead. But the will of God is not *always* about doing. It is, however, *always* about becoming, about learning, and about growing in our trust of God.

In the Scriptures we see that storms represent a couple of different ways that God acts in our lives. Sometimes there are storms of correction and sometimes there are storms of perfection. In the case of the prophet Jonah—a man who rebelled against God, refused to go where God told him to go, boarded a ship headed in the opposite direction, got caught in a storm, was thrown overboard, and was swallowed by a large fish—his storm was a storm of correction. God used the storm to correct Jonah in the same way a loving parent would correct an errant child. With the disciples, Jesus was using a storm of perfection to develop their trust in Him and cause it to mature.

Jesus decided He wanted to get away from the crowds and go over to the other side of the lake. Some of the disciples owned boats and were probably thinking, "We're professional fishermen. We make our living out here on the water. We know this lake like the back of our hands. We can handle this." They might have even said to their Master, "Jesus, You sit here in the back of the boat, take a nap, and we'll get you over to the other side of the lake safely. Do not worry about a thing. We've got it all under control."

And it was then that the carpenter took the fishermen for a little boat ride. As I said, trusting Christ does not always mean it will be smooth sailing. Isn't it true that God sometimes takes us into the territory we are most familiar with, the one we think we have the most control over, and then stirs it up, shaking it from top to bottom so that we'll learn just how foolish it is to think we are in control?

It is during those times of stormy weather that we are humbled from our arrogance and come to recognize how much we really need the Lord in our lives. That appears to have been the lasting impression this event had on the lives of Jesus' disciples. As they recounted this experience years later in the New Testament books, I find it interesting that they did not dress it up with a bunch of yardarm spin to make themselves look better. They could have told it more like this: "You should have seen us! The wind was blowing, the boat was filling up, and we were all paddling as hard as we could. Things were looking grim, but then our Master, Jesus, woke up, and He threw in with us. It was an awesome night that we'll never forget! We survived the perfect storm of '28!"

No, Matthew, Mark, and Luke are all pretty honest about the fact that on that day the disciples completely panicked. This was no legendary seafaring tale. The disciples were humble enough to tell us about their real fear during this real storm.

Jesus was tired, having had a couple demanding days healing lepers, casting out demons, preaching, and teaching. In spite of the miracles that He as the Son of God performed, Jesus was also human. He got tired, and so He fell asleep while the disciples began to move the boats across the lake.

All of a sudden, a violent storm rose up. Mark says, "There arose a fierce gale of wind, and the waves were breaking over the boat so much that the boat was already filling up" (4:37). In Matthew's account of this event, we are told "there arose a great storm on the sea" (8:24). The Greek word used here for *storm* is *sisemos*. It can be used to refer to a tempest, such as a gale-force wind above the sea, or to a violent shaking within the sea. If the word refers here to an earthquake underneath the lake, a tremor like this would have caused a phenomenon similar to holding a large bowl of water in your hands while trying to run with it, the bowl shaking, the water rocking from side to side and spilling all over the place.

Evidently, the waves became so massive that they were breaking over the top of the boat. At the same time there was also a storm in the sky above the waves. The wind was blowing at gale force, and it was nighttime, so it was pitch-black out. I can imagine the disciples had to be shocked and caught off guard. As their boat was filling with water, their hearts were filling with fear. This was it. They were going to die. Their ship was going down. They could see their lives flashing before their eyes.

Mark tells us there were other boats along that night. I can imagine the people in those boats thinking back to the miracles they had seen Jesus do earlier that day. They were probably bemoaning the fact that Jesus had not sailed with them! And this brings up the second thing this passage teaches us.

Trusting Christ Does Mean We Always Have Someone to Turn To

What is the best thing to do when you are afraid? Get around someone who isn't. Here I have another confession to make. When I was just a little boy, there were times I was afraid of the dark. My mom would tuck me in, turn off the light in my room, and close the door, and on many nights, from the very first minute I would see all kinds of monsters and goblins in the shadows from the window. It did not take long for me to jump up and go running down the hall to my mom's room so I could climb in bed and snuggle up next to her. She could protect me. She was not afraid, and being next to her calmed my fears.

The disciples finally figured this basic principle out, too. They were afraid, and so they turned to Jesus. And what does Mark tell us Jesus was doing? That's right—He was asleep. The only guy that could help them was catching some z's. That's like when the plane is going down and the pilot is out cold!

Do you ever think, "My ship's going down, and God's asleep at the wheel"? Do you ever wonder where God is when you are going through a storm like this? I have, too. So did the disciples that day. In Mark 4:38 you can almost hear the disciples screaming: "*Teacher, do You not care that we are perishing*?" And when the disciples finally turn to Him, Jesus is there for them.

I am not a parent, but I am impressed with those people who are. They can go to a party at a friend's house with their baby, set the baby on a bed in the guest room to sleep, go down and join the party with all of the music, laughing, and storytelling; but if their baby makes one little "waaaaa!" the parents can hear right through all the other noise and tell that it is their child's cry. I believe that in spite of the fury of the storm in your life, no matter how much confusion rages, when you cry, "Lord, have mercy!" it never falls on deaf ears. He can hear your cries. He knows what you are going through. You can always turn to Him.

This storm did not bother Jesus at all. He slept right through it. I am convinced Jesus knew the storm was coming. As a matter of fact, He may even have arranged it and then used it to develop the disciples' faith in Him.

Notice the response of Jesus after the disciples finally came to Him. Jesus asked them, "Why are you afraid? How is it that you have no faith?" (Mark 4:40). Ever the Master Teacher, Jesus was connecting the dots for the disciples. He wanted them to see that their lives depended ultimately not on their boat, not on their sailing skills, not on the weather, but on their trust in Him.

When Jesus rebuked the winds and the sea, they became perfectly calm. Mark says that Jesus told the storm, "Hush, be still." The Greek word is *phimoo*, and it means literally "Be muzzled." In effect, Jesus said to the storm, "Put a lid on it!" or "Zip it!" And Mark reports that "the wind died down and it became perfectly calm" (4:39). Upon Jesus' command, the earthquake (if that was part of the phenomenon) and the wind both subsided, and the sea became calm. With a storm that violent, in the natural order of things it would have taken hours for the sea to stop rocking back and forth and the waves to calm down.

In this memorable event, the disciples saw Jesus do something no ordinary person could do. He controlled nature. And this brings me to the third thing I see in this passage.

Trusting Christ Is Always Well-Placed Confidence

A child once prayed, "Dear Jesus, please help Mommy and Daddy. Take care of big sister and me. And please, God, take care of Yourself 'cause if anything ever happens to You, we're all in BIG trouble. Amen!"

Profound insight from such a young mind. Not that anything could ever "happen" to God, but the prayer is profound in the recognition that we are all utterly dependent on God. The apostle Paul, speaking about this same Jesus, tells us that "by Him all things were created, both in the heavens and on earth, visible and invisible, whether thrones or dominions or rulers or authorities—all things have been created through Him and for Him. He is before all things, and in Him all things hold together" (Colossians 1:16-17).

In other words, Jesus is one with God, and Jesus created everything and even holds everything together by His mighty power. Reminding ourselves of this is one of the best ways to encourage ourselves to trust in the Lord. Studying God's Word and reflecting back on all the times when God showed Himself to be both capable and faithful to His people builds confidence in our hearts and gives rise to a tenacious trust in God.

The point I would like to make from the story of the disciples on the stormy sea is that Jesus was contrasting fear of storms with trust in Him. As disciples ourselves, we may choose to listen to our fears and thereby silence our trust in Christ, or we may choose to trust in Christ and begin to silence our fears. Fear says "This storm is too big" and that we are destined to go down, as pawns of chance in a godless world. Trust says that even though there is a real storm raging, the real God who is there is really able to deliver us.

He can bring us through the storm. We may get drenched, we may even drown, but ultimately we place our confidence in the One who created the sky and the sea and everything in this world. He is the One we trust with our lives.

Trust—A Habit of the Heart

Trust is not a one-time thing. It is not just a past event. We do not say, "I trusted God on May 20, 1976," as if that were the end of it all. You may have begun to trust God on May 20, 1976, but now you must learn to trust Him as a way of life—daily, moment by moment. It must become a habit of heart and mind for all of us. We must learn to trust Him in the calm weather so that when we encounter the stormy weather, we are not caught off guard.

This is precisely what the disciples were beginning to see. Mark tells us that after the storm subsided, the disciples became even *more* afraid. Sounds as though they were taking a step backward, doesn't it? But there is a fear that leads us to be afraid, and there is another that leads us to awe, respect, and wonder. One is an unhealthy fear, the other a healthy one. The disciples were afraid (unhealthy fear) of the storm, but they now feared (healthy fear) Jesus.

This person in their boat had just performed a miracle in which He had controlled the vaster forces of nature. They had seen bodies healed, lepers cleansed, blind eyes opened, but up to this point, they had not seen anything like this, and it utterly blew their minds. Who was this Jesus, that even the wind and the sea obeyed Him? This is clearly what Jesus wanted them to think about. Through unique events like this, Jesus continued to establish in their minds exactly who He was: the very Son of God, the One who loved them, cared for them, and had come to rescue them. More than anything else, Jesus wanted them to learn they could trust Him.

The disciples began this story fearing the storm and ended it fearing the Lord. Which teaches us a great life principle: *When you have a healthy fear of God, you do not need to have an unhealthy fear of anything else.*

Throughout the Scriptures, one of the most-often-repeated commands given by God or an angel who represents God is, "Do not fear." God, speaking through the prophet Isaiah, reminds us,

> Do not fear, for I am with you;
> Do not anxiously look about you, for I am your God.
> I will strengthen you, surely I will help you,
> Surely I will uphold you with My righteous right hand (41:10).

And again,

> Do not fear, for I have redeemed you;
> I have called you by name; you are Mine!
> When you pass through the waters, I will be with you;
> And through the rivers, they will not overflow you (43:1-2).

At the same time, the Scriptures are replete with commands for us to fear the Lord. Is this a contradiction? Not at all. Because of our sinfulness, we are inherently afraid of God. We are anxious and afraid of what will happen when God judges us, afraid that He will one day find us out. That is why Adam and Eve ran and hid from God after they first sinned. They were ashamed, and they were afraid of God. But the God of the Bible is not interested in a bunch of cowering, frightened children who run away from Him in fear for their lives. On the contrary, Jesus was showing the disciples on the stormy sea that He was eager to have them come running to Him. Run to Him when you are in a storm. Run to Him when you have sinned. Run to Him when you are confused. He is eager to have you trust Him.

When Fear Leads to Trust

There is a sense in which the things we fear are actually the things we trust. When the disciples thought their ship was going down, the reason they were afraid is because they thought if they lost their ship, then *all* was lost. Their trust was in their ship. But

Jesus wanted them to place their trust in Him. We must learn to place our trust and confidence in the Lord, not in the things that are in this world. Ultimately, our jobs cannot save us, our relationships cannot save us, our health, wealth, popularity, and power cannot save us. God alone can save us. God alone is worthy of our ferocious trust.

Trusting God is not just about trusting Him to save us for eternity. It is also about trusting Him in the present moment, in today's weather, whether it be stormy or calm. Fearing the Lord is a handsome habit of heart, and the benefits of fearing the Lord are numerous, we are told. "The fear of the LORD is the beginning of knowledge." "The fear of the LORD leads to life; so that one may sleep satisfied, untouched by evil" (Proverbs 1:7, 19:23). Finally, in Proverbs 14:26-27 we are told, "In the fear of the LORD there is strong confidence, and his children will have refuge. The fear of the LORD is a fountain of life, that one may avoid the snares of death."

What tremendous promises—promises that can fuel our trust in God! This is not simply blind optimism. Optimism is based on temperament and mood; trust results in hope. As believers, our hope is based not on the mood of the moment but in placing our trust and confidence in the infinite, personal God and what He has said in His Word. God knows about the storms in your life, and He can use them to develop your trust in Him. Trusting Christ does not always mean smooth sailing, but trusting Christ does mean we always have Someone to turn to, and trusting Christ is always well-placed confidence.

Trust Leads to Peace

Isn't it true that when you live through a storm like these disciples did, you lean harder into God? Do not experiences like this draw you closer to the Lord? How many times have you seen the Lord take what was a negative and transform it into a positive?

A wise man once said, "There are many things in life that will catch your eye, but only a few will catch your heart....Pursue those." That is what happened to these disciples of Jesus. He caught their hearts that day on the stormy sea, and all but one of them trusted Him for the rest of their lives.

Christian spirituality does not offer a simple solution to a complicated problem; it is not just "Don't worry. Be happy!" It is "Don't worry. Trust God. He is in control. He will take care of you." The peace that God gives to Christ's disciples is not the absence of trouble, but rather the confidence that when you walk through a storm, He will walk with you, and whenever you need to, you can turn to Him. His calming presence will always be with you.

Thomas à Kempis said:

> To preserve peace in time of trouble our will must remain firm in God and be ever directed towards Him, that is, we should be disposed to receive all things from the hand of God, from His justice, and from His bounty, with humble submission to His blessed will. Good and evil, health and sickness, prosperity and adversity, consolation and dryness, temptation and tranquility, interior sweetness, trials and chastisements, all should be received by the soul with humility, patience, and resignation, as coming to us by the appointment of God. This is the only means of finding peace in the midst of great troubles and adversity.

Remain firm in God. Direct your heart and mind toward Him. Find your peace in the fact that He is trustworthy and is always in control.

There was a story in the devotional magazine *Our Daily Bread* a few years ago that told of a group of scientists and botanists who were exploring remote regions of the Alps in search of new species of flowers. One day they noticed through their binoculars a flower of such rarity and beauty that its value to science was incalculable. Unfortunately, it was down in a tight ravine with steep cliffs on both sides. To get the flower, someone very small would have to be lowered down the cliff on a rope.

A curious young boy was watching nearby, and the scientists told him they would pay him well if he would agree to be lowered over the cliff to retrieve the flower below.

The boy took a long look down into the ravine and said, "I'll be back in a minute." A short time later he returned, followed by a gray-haired man. Approaching the botanists, the boy said, "I'll go down there and get that flower for you if this man holds the rope. He's my dad."

King David said, "When I am afraid, I will put my trust in You" (Psalm 56:3). When you trust someone, it is not because you control the outcome. Trust is not always accompanied by knowledge. Sometimes I have no idea what God is up to in my life. Sometimes, I simply have to trust that getting into His presence is the answer.

Trust grows in a relationship over time. The longer I walk with the Lord, the more I am convinced He is trustworthy. God is the One I can turn to, the One I can trust to hold the rope or get me through the storm.

- *Is doubt a sin?*
- *Can you be a believer and still have doubts?*
- *What is the best way to go about handling doubt?*
- *Where can we go for answers to our questions and doubts?*
- *How does God feel about our doubts?*

10
How Should We Handle Doubt?

Doubt is not always a sign that a man is wrong; it may be a sign that he is thinking.

OSWALD CHAMBERS

What Is in a Name?

In case you had not noticed, my last name is Thomas. It is the name given me by my immediate ancestors, but it has also long been attached to and joined with the word *doubting* when talking about those who struggle with belief.

It is safe to say that I live up to my name in regard to both of these uses. There are things about me that remind people of the Thomases who have gone before me: my father, grandfather, and other Thomas family members. And there have also been times when my heart and mind were racked by the riddles of life, making it feel as though my faith was choking in a smoke cloud of skepticism.

The moniker "Doubting Thomas" stems from the first century, when a newly resurrected Jesus Christ showed up at a meeting of some of His disciples. Unfortunately, the one named Thomas was not there that night. Later, when the disciples told Thomas the good news about having seen Jesus alive again, the incredulous Thomas (who was more of a "seeing is believing" kind of guy) told them, "Unless I shall see in His hands the imprint of the nails, and put my finger into the place of the nails, and put my hand into His side, I will not believe" (John 20:25).

The truth, I have learned, is that even when I am living up to that side of my Thomas name, I am not alone. As a matter of fact, according to the Bible, I am in some pretty good company. Within its pages I have discovered many people of faith who had moments of doubt. It all started in the beginning with Adam and Eve doubting what God had said about the consequences of eating from the Tree of the Knowledge of Good and Evil. They doubted God, picked the fruit, ate it, and the world has not been the same since. Doubt is also evident in the lives of people like Abraham, Moses, Gideon, King David, Elijah, and many others, who all went through periods of questioning, but nonetheless would all easily qualify for induction into the Hall of Fame for Giants of the Faith.

Most of us have experienced doubts about God. They bring on thoughts such as, *If God would just make Himself visible, then all my doubts would disappear.* But then it dawns on you that even though God walked the earth in the Person of Jesus Christ, living right there in front of humanity, preaching, teaching, and working miracles, there were still those who struggled with doubt.

Thomas was one of them. As one of the original 12 disciples, he had seen Jesus heal people, calm storms, raise the dead, and walk on water right before his very eyes. Yet Thomas still had doubts. It is fair to deduce then that belief in God and acceptance of the Christian faith is not something that you do once for all and then you are done with it. Christian faith is an everyday affair. It was never meant to be a static, intellectual acquiescence, but rather a dynamic belief based on a living relationship.

Maintaining faith is not that much different from having to tune my guitar. Though they tuned it at the factory and the guys at the store where I bought it tuned it again, that was not the end of it. I still have to tune the guitar on a regular basis if it is to play correctly. And there is something called "concert pitch," which serves as the standard to which I must tune my guitar if it is to play in true tune. So, too, belief must be maintenanced if it is to remain "in tune." And just as I make adjustments on my guitar to get it to concert pitch, there is a living Absolute to whom I must adjust my beliefs if I am to be in tune with *truth*.

How about you? Do you also have times when all this talk about God, Jesus, sin, salvation, and heaven just seems like a bunch of hot air? Do you ever find it just a little too much to believe? If so, I want you to know you are not alone; you are not crazy. If anything, you are at least as normal as I am (that is *supposed* to be a comforting thought).

One significant New Testament personality who learned this was John the Baptist. John, usually considered the last of the Old Testament prophets, was very close to Jesus. They were even relatives and most likely played together as young boys. Yet John the Baptist still struggled with doubts. I think we can learn a lot by looking at his life and his "bout with doubt."

It is important for you to know that John the Baptist probably would not have fit well in an ad for Abercrombie and Fitch, Gap, Eddie Bauer, or Banana Republic. He was a scruffy kind of guy, an outdoorsy type. We are told that he wore camel's-hair clothes, lived out in the desert, and ate wild locusts and honey. John probably had a matted, sticky beard full of locust shells and grasshopper wings.

Matthew's Gospel tells us that John preached in the wilderness area of Judea; the essence of John's message was the same as that of Jesus: "Repent, for the kingdom of heaven is at hand" (see Matthew 3:1-12).

John's message may have been simple, but it was powerful. We are told that while he was preaching and baptizing, John attracted huge crowds, including some of the religious leaders from Jerusalem—and those guys did not go out to hear just *anybody*. But John was like a spiritual lightning bolt. He offended almost everyone and spoke the truth like nobody had for quite some time.

John did not hesitate to "call it like he saw it" when he compared the religious leaders of his time to a bunch of snakes. No one had ever done that. The Pharisees, scribes, and Sadducees were revered as the most holy and religious men around, and yet here came this scruffy, uneducated, ragamuffin preacher, John the Baptizer, scolding them like whipped puppies. Then, to add insult to insult, John told the religious leaders that their judgment was right around the corner. He told them that the Messiah would come soon and execute judgment on them, bringing them down because of their fruitless faith and self-righteous hypocrisy.

The highlight of John's ministry was the day he had the privilege of baptizing Jesus (see Matthew 3:13-17). John knew Jesus was the Messiah, the One whose arrival he had been sent to announce. Matthew tells us:

> After being baptized, Jesus came up immediately from the water; and behold, the heavens were opened, and he saw the Spirit of God descending as a dove, and lighting on Him, and behold, a voice out of the heavens, said, "This is My beloved Son, in whom I am well-pleased" (Matthew 3:16-17).

I do not know about you, but that never happened to me at church camp. We had some great moments singing around the campfire, but certainly nothing like that! I would love to have been there to hear that voice out of heaven. You would think that anyone who had been there that day would never have had another doubt about God or Jesus. I mean, seeing and hearing is believing, right?

Wrong.

When we pick up John's story a few months later, he has been locked up in a dark and damp prison cell.

Why was John in prison? Mark's Gospel tells us that John had openly rebuked King Herod for having an adulterous relationship with his own brother's wife, Herodias. Of course it is never safe to publicly scold an Eastern despot. But John the Baptist was not one to shrink back from the duties of a prophet.

Plus, John probably expected that Jesus had come to break him out of prison. After all, the Messiah had come to set up His kingdom, right? Surely, freeing John would be high on the Messiah's "Things to Do" list.

But sitting there in that damp and lonely prison for a day, then a week, then a month, and as some have suggested, as much as a year, what do you think was going on in John's mind? Matthew tells us:

> Now when John [the Baptist], while imprisoned, heard of the works of Christ, he sent word by his disciples and said to Him, "Are You the Expected One, or shall we look for someone else?" (Matthew 11:2-3).

Notice Matthew's use of the word *Christ* here. It is most intentional. Matthew wants us to know who it is that John is having doubts about. He is having doubts about Jesus, the same person he had baptized that day with all the fanfare from heaven, the same one he really believed was the Messiah.

Now, if Matthew's Gospel was written to convince us all to believe in Jesus, why in the world would he include an account like this in his book? I mean, this is the story of how John, a great man of faith, struggled with doubts about whether Jesus was the Christ.

This is one of the reasons I love the Bible so much. It is honest and realistic. John doubted, and Matthew did not try to spin it. He did not try to hide it. He was honest about it. God knew that you and I might have questions and doubts, that sometimes our lives feel like we are trapped in some prison, with little to no hope of getting out, feeling as though God is ignoring our circumstances and refusing to come to our rescue. He knew that some of us would have intellectual questions about our faith that would twist our minds into all kinds of contortions, wondering whether God even exists, or if He does, whether He hears our prayers, whether He knows the things we are feeling as we go through those dark nights of the soul.

And so God inspired Matthew to tell the *whole* truth, to include this account, to remind you and me that we are not that much different from one of the greatest people of faith who ever lived: John the Baptist.

The Doubts of a Prophet

I wonder if there have been times in your life when God did not perform as you had expected. Were there times when you thought you had been completely forgotten by Him, moments when your faith seemed as thin as a spider's web, so fragile you feared it would not be able to hold the weight of your doubts? Or maybe you made some move in your life thinking you were doing the right thing—just what God wanted you to do—and then something went wrong and blew up in your face, causing you to ask, "God, didn't I hear You correctly on this?"

Unfortunately, most of us have not had the benefit of hearing a voice from heaven like John did. But the point is that even if we did, would we be able to build a lifetime of unwavering faith on a one-time experience? I think it is incredibly important that you and I notice that John the Baptist could not keep from wavering. And if John could not, I do not think you and I can either.

As we see from John's life, the strength of our faith is not found in ourselves. It is not about how much faith we have in terms of volume or quantity. It is not about drumming up a level of emotional confidence. It is not about setting your mind on a fixed course and refusing all doubt. It is more often about having a humble and honest heart, one that admits its weakness and looks to God for refreshment and strength. It is about recognizing that the *object* of our faith (Jesus) is also the *Source* of our faith (see Hebrews 12:2).

What to Do with Your Doubts

So what did John the Baptist do with his doubts? First, he clarified the core questions. Sometimes when we are going through a period of doubt, it is hard to put a finger on what it is we're questioning. That is why it is good to do what John did. He reduced whatever feelings of doubt he had down to the question about whether or not Jesus was the promised Messiah.

Your questions might be altogether different from John's, but it will still help if you stop, take a few minutes, and figure out exactly what it is you are doubting. Is it the truthfulness of the Bible? Is it whether or not God exists? Is it a question about hypocrisy in the church? Or are you wrestling with whether or not something you are doing is forbidden in Scripture? Identifying your questions is an important first step.

Second, John took his questions straight to Jesus. Although he was in prison and could not go himself, he had his disciples take the questions directly to Jesus. He did not go to the local synagogue officials. He did not go to the local self-help clinic or call the Jerusalem Psychic Hotline. John went straight to Jesus.

Likewise, it is important to understand that God desires you to come to Him with your honest questions. The Christian faith is not a lifeless religion; it is a relationship with the living God. The Christian faith does not require you to go to an intermediary—some sort of spiritual guru or mystic philosopher. The Christian faith teaches us that you and I have direct access to the God of the universe, to whom we can both deliver our questions and ask for help.

Now please do not misunderstand me. I am not trying to say you should never talk with someone else about your doubts. There is much that can be gained from seeking the wise counsel of other people. But I *am* saying that biblical Christianity opens the door for you to take your honest questions right into the throne room of Almighty God. King David knew this well when in a moment of doubt and honest desperation, he prayed, "How long, O LORD? Will You forget me forever? How long will You hide Your face from me?" (Psalm 13:1).

Whenever you have doubts, no matter how intense they might seem, your best course of action is to clarify your core questions, and then go straight to God with them.

Do not worry too much about how you word your questions. David never did. He shook his fist at heaven all the time. He expressed deep doubts about God's love for him and about God's timing in bringing about the help he needed. And in this humble honesty before God, David was called a "man after God's own heart." What an honor to be remembered that way.

Finally, we should see our lives in the context of God's plans for us. This is what John the Baptist did. He knew that God had plans for his life that went way beyond his own imagination. He knew that the very God who was in charge of all of human history had a hand on his life.

We can trust the sovereign Lord of all with our doubts. He is not afraid of our questions; He is not insulted by our fears. God in His infinitude has numbered the very hairs of your head, and He knows what you are going through. The reason you are safe is because, in the end, you are in His hands.

How God Responds to Our Doubts

Matthew continues to describe what happened that day:

> Jesus answered and said to them, "Go and report to John what you hear and see: the BLIND RECEIVE SIGHT and the lame walk, the lepers are cleansed and the deaf hear, the dead are raised up, and the POOR HAVE THE GOSPEL PREACHED TO THEM" (Matthew 11:4-5; the words in small capitals are excerpted paraphrases from Isaiah 35 and 61).

How did Jesus answer John's questions? By pointing to the miracles He was performing and the message He was preaching. Both of these tied Jesus to Old Testament messianic prophecy. Jesus reminded John that the truth he was seeking had been revealed in Scripture. In the midst of John's doubts and troubles, it was the Word of the Lord that would sustain him.

King David also knew about the power of God's Word to sustain during tough times. Listen to how he put it:

> Deal bountifully with Your servant, that I may live and keep Your word. Open my eyes, that I may behold

> wonderful things from Your law. I am a stranger in the earth; do not hide Your commandments from me. My soul is crushed with longing after Your ordinances at all times. You rebuke the arrogant, the cursed, who wander from Your commandments. Take away reproach and contempt from me, for I observe Your testimonies. Even though princes sit and talk against me, Your servant meditates on Your statutes. Your testimonies also are my delight; they are my counselors (Psalm 119:17-24).

How much more is this true for us? We have the benefit of looking back through Scripture, both the Old Testament and the New Testament, and learning how these great people of faith struggled with doubt. In the midst of much worse life conditions than any of us will probably ever face, they came face-to-face with the giant of doubt. And what was it that sustained them? What was it that gave them comfort? The statutes of God and the testimonies of God's faithfulness. These became their counselors, words of comfort and peace that restored their confidence in God's love for them.

When we have periods of doubt, one of the best things we should do is one of the simplest things we can do: Read God's Word. Find a passage that speaks to the circumstances with which you are wrestling. Find a narrative passage that describes how someone else dealt with a similar situation.

Read it once, and then read it again. Meditate on it. Pray and ask the Holy Spirit to reveal its words of hope to you. In humility, invite the Lord to open the eyes of your heart and show you how His Word can be a lamp to *your* feet and a light to *your* path right here, right now.

Finishing the Race

John had an incredible start in faith, and Jesus counseled him by saying, "Do not give up now. Don't stumble by misunderstanding Me or My timing in bringing about My will for your life." I think that God has said the same thing to me, and perhaps

He is saying that to you right now for whatever doubts might be unsettling your mind and heart. Do not give up. Do not doubt in the dark what you knew to be true in the light. God will prove Himself to be faithful. The only question is, Will you trust Him?

Adam, Eve, Abraham, Moses, Gideon, King David, Elijah, John the Baptist, you, and me—all of us are believers and sometimes doubters. Our walk of faith reminds me of Derek Redmond. In the official record books of the 1992 Olympics, Derek Redmond's attempt in the semifinals of the men's 400-meter race is listed as "race abandoned." But as *USA Today's* Mike Dodd has said, "To 65,000 fans in Montjuic Olympic Stadium in Barcelona, Spain, and millions of television viewers, that's the most ironic misnomer in the history of the Games." I remember watching that race on television. It is one of those moments you just never forget. Redmond was 250 meters away from the finish line when he pulled a hamstring and fell down hard.

He knew he was not just another runner. He really had a chance at the medal. But then he fell down.

As the other runners blew past him, Redmond said that he thought to himself, "If I get up now and run, I can still qualify." He struggled to his feet, grimaced in pain, and stumbled forward several more feet. But then he fell down again.

By now, the other runners had all crossed the finish line. But as the cameras retrained their focus from the finish line to the runner who was once again rising to his feet, it became apparent that the race was far from over.

Seconds turned into minutes, almost in slow motion as Redmond took one step and then another. But to the horror of the watching world, it quickly became evident that he would never make it on his own.

Then all of a sudden, there was a stirring in the crowd. From somewhere near the top of the stands, another man came running down. He jumped over the concrete divider and headed toward the fallen Olympian. Arriving at the runner's side, he threw his arm around the young man's shoulder to support him. The young runner seemed dazed at first and tried to pull away, but the man would not let go. Then the man said to him, "Son, you don't have to do this. You've got nothing to prove." And Derek Redmond knew who it was that had come to his aid.

As Dodd reported their conversation, it went something like this:

> Derek recalled, "I told him I had to finish; I was going to finish the race."
>
> Then Jim Redmond, Derek's father said, "Well, we've started everything together. We'll finish this together."
>
> The two walked slowly all the way to the finish line together; all over the world, people did exactly what the 65,000 people in that stadium did that day...we stood with cheerful applause at the courage and perseverance of Derek Redmond who finished his race.

Doubt is a little like pulling a muscle in the middle of your race. Sometimes it hits you from out of nowhere, like being blindsided by a personal tragedy or finding out that one of the people you look up to is not all he or she appeared to be.

At other times, doubt can be the result of the slow atrophy of your faith, like when a muscle has not been used in a while. Spiritual atrophy happens when we do not spend time with the Father, meditate on God's Word, pray more than just crisis prayers, give ourselves away in service, or focus our hearts in true and spiritual worship of God.

John the Baptist had fallen into doubt when he was not very far from the finish line. And the Father, looking down from heaven, made sure that he got the encouraging news he needed. Jesus was indeed the Coming One.

Frederick Buechner has said, "Whether your faith is that there is a God or that there is not a God, if you do not have any doubts you are either kidding yourself or asleep."[1] Let's not try to fool ourselves, God, or each other. Let's be honest about doubt. And above all, let's not be guilty of falling down and then just falling asleep where we fell. Let's keep our faith moving.

If you are going through a period of doubt, consider yourself among those of us who fall down once in awhile. To doubt is not to sin. Honest doubt is one thing, willful disbelief is quite another. One is sincerity; the other is obstinacy. One hungers for light; the other falls asleep in the dark.

Take courage. Your doubts could just be a sign that you are thinking, and your faith is getting ready to start moving again. And remember to do what John the Baptist did: Clarify your core questions, take them straight to God, then begin to see your life as a part of God's overall plan. Finally, go to God's Word for light and guidance.

Then you can say with David:

> I have chosen the faithful way; I have placed Your ordinances before me. I cling to Your testimonies; O LORD, do not put me to shame! I shall run the way of Your commandments, for You will enlarge my heart (Psalm 119:30-32).

- *If God is both good and all-powerful, then why does He allow all of the evil, pain, suffering, and death in the world?*
- *Why do bad things happen to good people and good things happen to bad people?*
- *Where is God when life hurts?*
- *Can we find meaning or purpose in our pain or make any sense out of all the tragedy in this life?*

11

Why Does God Allow So Much Pain and Suffering?

When pain is to be borne, a little courage helps more than much knowledge, a little human sympathy more than much courage, and the least tincture of the love of God more than all.

C.S. Lewis

Horatio G. Spafford was a successful Chicago businessman who, at the age of 43, suffered a major financial setback due to the Great Chicago Fire of 1871. He and his wife were still reeling from the recent death of their son and so, after the fire, Spafford decided the family needed to get away for a while. His good friend D.L. Moody was about to hold a series of evangelistic crusades in England, so Spafford and his wife decided to book passage on a ship to take the family over and join Moody.

At the very last minute, Spafford had to stay behind to attend to some unexpected business developments, but he sent his wife and four daughters on ahead, planning to follow as soon as he could.

On November 22, as their ship, the *S.S. Ville du Havre,* was crossing the Atlantic, it was struck by an English vessel called the *Lochearn.* The *Ville du Havre* sank in just 12 minutes, and 226 lives were lost. When the survivors landed at Cardiff, Wales, Mrs. Spafford sent this cable message to her husband: "Saved alone."

Spafford booked passage on the very next ship to go and join his grieving wife. As he crossed the Atlantic, the captain pointed out the place where the *Ville du Havre* had gone down. That night, Spafford penned these words to a now-famous hymn of the faith:

> When peace like a river attendeth my way,
> When sorrows like sea-billows roll;
> Whatever my lot, Thou hast taught me to say,
> "It is well, it is well, with my soul."

In short duration, Spafford suffered the loss of his son, financial ruin in the great fire, and then the loss of his four daughters. Humanly speaking, it is almost impossible to imagine how anyone could find peace in the midst of such a relentless string of tragedies. What was it that Horatio Spafford held onto during those times of such great personal pain and loss? What was it he believed in so strongly that gave him such invincible hope?

The subject of pain, evil, and suffering has been the study of philosophers and theologians for centuries. The question of why God allows pain and suffering has probably crossed your mind as well. Most likely it arose when you or someone you know was going through some kind of tragedy or painful experience. That's when we are most likely to ask the big "why" questions: "*Why* did this happen? Why did this happen to *me?* Why did this happen *now?*" And that is when we are most desperate to find some meaning behind our suffering.

It may not lessen anyone's pain to point out that the problem of pain is not a new issue. Even when we look to the Bible, we read that Jesus said to His followers, "In the world you have tribulation, but take courage; I have overcome the world" (John 16:33). You will notice that Jesus did not say *if* you have tribulation. He said you *will* have tribulation. However, according to Jesus, while pain is a given, misery is optional. When tribulation comes in this world, Jesus said we could take courage because He has overcome the world.

At this point, someone may say, "That's nice, but could you help me see precisely *how* Jesus' overcoming the world will help me?

Why doesn't God just wave His magic wand over the world and end all the evil, pain, and suffering? How are we supposed to find the silver lining behind some of these massive thunderclouds?"

To be sure, pain is everywhere, and it comes in all shapes and sizes. Pain comes wrapped in earthquakes, tornadoes, flooding, disease, drunk-driving accidents, high school gunfire, church burnings, divorce, political corruption, and so on. It seems indiscriminate about who its victims are. Babies and children are not innocent or cute enough to escape its reach, marriages are not sacred enough, churches and synagogues are not holy enough, post offices and other government buildings are not protected enough. Pain can walk through any door, anywhere, at any time, and pull the rug out from under even the safest of the safe.

Two Kinds of Pain

The first thing we should realize is that there are at least two general categories of pain: physiological and psychological. The first manifests itself in physical pain, as when you smash your finger with a hammer or break your leg. The second category of pain is experienced in the mental and emotional realm when, for example, you are afraid of something or your heart is broken by some kind of loss or missed opportunity. Both kinds of pain come in a variety of intensities. It is one thing to burn your finger and quite another to lose a limb. It is one thing to flunk a math test and quite another to lose a job. Sometimes people experience both kinds of pain at the same time, such as when they make a trip to the dentist or have to go to war to defend their country.

Eventually, everyone experiences both kinds of pain. You have probably had one of those days—you know, where everything that *can* go wrong, *does* go wrong. Did one of those days ever turn into one of those weeks? Did that week ever turn into one of those months or years? And did it ever begin to look like it was on its way to becoming one of those lives? If so, then you know what I mean about the universality of pain.

My wife claims to be a natural klutz. She says she cannot walk through a store without bumping into something and knocking several items off the shelves. She experiences pain almost daily and bears the proof in the scars on her hand from while she was cutting the pumpkin, scars on her knees from banging into table legs at restaurants, and a scar on her lip from knocking over a microphone stand, stepping on the base of the stand, and then watching in horror as the microphone came back at her like the proverbial stepped-on rake.

Of course these kinds of physical pain are minor compared to what some people have to deal with. There are people who have to cope with debilitating amounts of physical pain every minute of their lives.

Psychological pain is no stranger to most of us either. We have experienced this kind of pain when we take a trip to the doctor, are unsettled by a series of midterm exams, or become tied up in knots at employee review time. The scars of psychological pain include the relational dysfunctions of adult children of alcoholics, the increasing divorce rate, and the exponential growth in the sale of mood-altering drugs.

Emotional pain can be quite traumatic for those who live under the tyranny of a verbally abusive spouse, sibling, or parent. Being told you are a "dummy" and that you "never do anything right" can inflict a devastating amount of pain on the human spirit. Scars of the soul run deep, and the light of life can fade from the eyes of anyone who has received the brunt of lifelong psychological pain.

Looking for Hope

There are really two approaches to the discussion of pain. One is intellectual and the other existential. One deals with theories and the other with experiences. A meaningful treatment of the subject must include both aspects. To talk about pain, suffering, and evil on a purely philosophical level would be fine for those who like to chase such things around, but it would leave out some of the richest thoughts ever heard on the subject. And yet, to focus only on personal experiences might make us feel better for a moment or two, but then would leave us with nothing to anchor our minds and hearts to when the pain or the memory of it returns.

Besides, the very reasons people are interested in the subject of pain are also both intellectual and existential. They either have experienced some great amount of pain and are trying to make sense out of it, or they are afraid they will soon experience pain and are preparing in advance to take the hit. So, if we are to understand pain at all, we must grapple with it intellectually and then take a look at the role pain plays in the real world of our lives.

The Intellectual Problem of Pain

You might be among those who have taken a philosophy course somewhere along the way which taught that, if God exists, He is either unwilling or unable to do something about the evil and suffering in this world. Otherwise, He would surely have done away with all that by now. You might have had discussions centering on questions like, "Why would a good God allow the horrors of the Holocaust, the scourges of disease, the death and destruction of war? If He has the power, then why didn't He prevent them from happening in the first place?" I believe these are honest questions which deserve honest answers.

We can learn something from the very fact that pain exists. You see, pain can only have meaning if there is something more to this world than just chemicals and atoms. That is, if you are an atheist and you believe that the physical universe is all there is, then you really have no right to complain about the existence or injustice of pain. For the consistent atheist, painful experiences are just the result of time plus chance, accidental collocations of elements of the physical universe. For the true atheist, there is no such thing as finding meaning in what amounts to the natural movements of an impersonal world.

The atheist has both a harder and an easier time explaining the existence of pain than the Christian. If the atheist is talking about the *cause* of pain, the explanation can be that when pain is experienced, it is a result of the movements of various elements of the physical universe. No real intellectual problem exists from this vantage point. Everything is mechanistic because everything is meaningless.

But the moment an atheist begins talking about the outrage or injustice of pain or the significance and meaning a person might find in painful experiences, the atheist has begun to cheat on atheism. For the atheist to remain consistent, he or she is forced to admit that the death of a child is as ultimately meaningless as the falling of a rock into the ocean.

The Christian has a much more difficult job in talking about the cause of pain, especially as it relates to the existence of a good and all-powerful God. But Christians do have the upper hand in that they can talk about the injustice of pain and about how to find meaning in pain, which the atheist cannot.

The existence of pain is one of the favorite intellectual arguments of the atheist and perhaps the most formidable. The issue is a difficult one to deal with, no matter how you approach it. A case can be made that the existence of pain suggests the universe is a dangerous and evil place in which to live. From the very day you were born, you began to die, as though life itself were just a cruel joke—a joke set in play either by "chance" or some kind of sadomasochistic deity who enjoys watching us writhe and squirm our way from birth all the way to the grave.

While this hopeless response is often presented as though it were the *only* solution to the philosophical problem of pain, the issue is not so simply dealt with. The existence of one thing does not disprove the existence of another, nor does it necessarily determine the characteristics of another thing. The existence of pain really says nothing about the existence or character of God. It is not any sort of explicit contradiction to say, "God exists" and also to say, "Pain exists." A contradiction would be if I were to say "God exists" and "God does not exist," or "Pain exists," and "Pain does not exist." The real question is, How do we make sense out of the coexistence of the two?

Is there a good answer? How can we reconcile the existence of a good and all-powerful God with a meaningful answer to the problem of pain? Part of the answer may be found in uncovering a distorted view of what is meant by the terms *all-powerful* and *good* when we talk about God.

The All-Powerful God

If by *all-powerful* we mean that God can do anything at all, then we are not talking about the Christian idea of God. Anything at all would have to include the ability to create a square circle, a round triangle, a married bachelor, a male daughter, or any number of other absolute impossibilities. If the words *square* and *circle* have any meaning at all, then God cannot create a square circle.

A common question that is asked is, "If God can do *anything*, can God make a rock so big that He couldn't pick it up?" A similar logical conundrum is, "What happens when an unstoppable force meets an immovable object?" In both cases we are dealing with mutually exclusive alternatives which lead to absolute impossibilities. God is the name of the Being who is truly supreme, and nothing can be greater than God. God cannot create a rock or anything else that would then be greater than Himself, and which would thereby stop Him from being who He is. As for the second question, if there were such a thing as an unstoppable force, there could be no such thing as an immovable object and vice versa. The existence of one negates the existence of the other. Both of these questions are nonsensical because they are dealing with absolute impossibilities.

God is all-powerful, and this means that anything that can be done can be done by God. God can create from out of nothing, manage the universe, divide the heavens from the earth, and raise the dead. There is nothing God cannot do except stop being God.

The Goodness of God

The second thing we need to clarify is what we mean when we say that God is good. If *good* means that God exists to meet our every whim, like a spiritual Santa Claus, then we are not talking about the Christian idea of God at all. When Christians say that God is good, we mean that God has our highest good in mind, that He is benevolent, and that He intends for us to live life to its fullest, experiencing the kind of spiritual growth that will enable us to reflect His image into a world which is full of darkness.

Those who think of God as a magic genie whose only mission is to secure our amusement and happiness have missed the point altogether. God will not sacrifice our holiness for our happiness. Our greatest good, as defined by God, is not about job opportunities, romantic encounters, or a bulging savings account. In and of themselves, these things are not bad. But sometimes we make the mistake of thinking our greatest good is tied directly to these kinds of things. In God's economy, however, our greatest good has more to do with personal holiness and opportunities to accurately reflect God's glory in our world.

One element of God's plan for our greatest good is that we should have free will. With that free will, God has set it up that we can choose to do right or wrong and that there will be consequences that attend our choices. God did not desire to make a world filled with automatons and robots who have no free will. He took the great risk of love and gave us the opportunity to choose or refuse His lordship in our lives. That necessarily leaves open the possibility that we will separate ourselves from God and from each other by the choices we make. When we do this, we leave ourselves open to the natural consequences which follow our selfishness.

Some people have suggested that it would have been better for God not to have given us free will. But as Augustine, one of the greatest philosopher-theologians of the Christian faith, put it, "As a runaway horse is better than a stone which does not run away because it lacks self-movement and sense perception, so the creature is more excellent which sins by free will than that which does not sin only because it has no free will."[1] And even more excellent is the creature who chooses not to sin in a response of love and gratitude to the almighty and good God.

That God is good does not always mean we will fully understand what God in His goodness intends for us. We are finite and affected by the Fall. Our concept of what is good for us is sure to be at times quite different from God's, but not so different as to render the word *good* meaningless, as if God's goodness were a complete opposite to our conception of goodness. As C.S. Lewis has put it:

> The Divine "goodness" differs from ours, but it is not sheerly different: it differs from ours not as white from black but as a perfect circle from a child's first attempt to draw a wheel. But when the child has learned to draw, it will know that the circle it then makes is what it was trying to make from the very beginning.[2]

This means we will not always understand how a good God would allow some of the struggles that we must face. But the further we go along in spiritual growth, the more clearly we see and understand God's dealings with us. He is about the business of improving us, never having been one to settle for the status quo. Like a master painter working on his or her paintings, God dabs, rubs, strokes, and brings into our lives those things which He deems are for our greater good.

The Cause of Pain

From the Christian perspective there is a single primary cause of pain in the world. Pain is a result of what theologians call the Fall of mankind. The Fall refers to the entrance of sin into the physical world, the intentional disregard for God's will which began with our first parents, Adam and Eve. This does not mean that Christians believe each and every specific incident of pain is a direct result of a specific sin, but that the reality of sin is the general cause behind all pain.

Through the Fall, humankind and all of creation have been polluted from the original state in which they were created. Because of Adam and Eve's disobedience, God pronounced a judgment on mankind which theologian Anthony Hoekema has pointed out was threefold.[3] This judgment is described in the third chapter of Genesis:

1. "Cursed is the ground because of you; in toil you will eat of it all the days of your life" (Genesis 3:17). Hoekema tells us that the word translated "toil" here is the same word as *pains*, used to describe the pains of childbirth. Before the Fall, Adam and Eve had enjoyed their work in the garden, but because of the Fall, physical work was now accompanied by pain and difficulty.

2. "Both thorns and thistles it shall grow for you" (Genesis 3:18). Because of the Fall, their labor to grow food to survive became inconvenienced by interruptions and setbacks. Many Bible scholars believe this part of the curse of the Fall extends beyond thorns and thistles, showing up in other aspects of nature such as floods, earthquakes, hurricanes, and diseases. This appears to be confirmed by Romans 8:21 when the apostle Paul tells us that the whole of creation groans to be "set free from its slavery to corruption." And so we have at least the suggestion that our struggle with nature and natural disasters has come as part of the consequences of the Fall.

3. "For you are dust, and to dust you shall return" (Genesis 3:19). Physical death is also a direct consequence of the Fall. Prior to the Fall, physical death did not exist. According to Genesis 5:5, Adam lived to the ripe old age of 930, and many other people back then lived multiple hundreds of years as well. Current life spans are much shorter than they were around the origin of mankind. This is likely a result of the compounding pollution of sinful deeds.

So for the Christian, the general cause of all pain stems directly or indirectly back to the Fall of mankind and the entrance of sin into the world. Before the Fall, things were as God had originally intended. Pain, struggling, and death were clearly not a part of human experience. After the Fall, pain, struggling, and death became a shocking reality for our ancestors and an inherited reality for us.

A World Without Pain?

Some people have asked the question, "Why couldn't God come up with another plan, a world where there didn't have to be any pain?"

From the Bible we know that God desired to make mankind with a moral free will. This means God decided to create us with the real opportunity to choose between right and wrong. He placed us in an environment that allowed for these choices to be exercised, accompanied by real consequences. These consequences, whether good or bad, whether pleasurable or painful, are the direct or indirect result of the right and wrong choices we make of our own free will. It would be self-contradictory for God to have created us with free will and then to coerce us into always making right choices in order that we would experience only good consequences. Therefore, it is reasonable for God to have made our world a place where pain exists and can actually occur.

In the world in which we live, we encounter both *natural laws* and *moral laws* which have been set up by God. Because this is so, our free moral choices now have real weight; they impact the amount of pain we experience and the amount of pain we might cause for people around us.

For instance, in the physical world God made mankind as air-breathing mammals. But if we were to try living underwater without the aid of breathing machinery, it would be logical to expect that we would come to some harm and possibly die. This is part of the natural law and covers the natural order of the physical world in which we live. When we go against natural law, we do not break just the natural law. We break ourselves against it.

The same thing is true with moral law. Since God has told us it is wrong for us to murder each other, lie to each other, commit adultery, and so on, our God-given moral significance necessarily includes the real option to choose wrong. So, if we were to choose to disobey God's moral law by committing adultery, we might very well ruin our marriages, causing pain to both ourselves and our spouses. Or if we were to hold another human being underwater for an extended period of time, we could, of our own free will, employ the natural law (which God set up) to break a moral law (which God also set up) and inflict real and fatal pain on another human being.

The freedom that comes with moral significance is a freedom that when respected can keep us relatively safe or, when disregarded, can cause us great harm. It would be an absolute impossibility to create a world in which creatures are given true free will and then only permit them to do that which is good so that their lives are completely pleasant.

The Existential Problem of Pain

Now let's move out of the realm of philosophy and ask some very hard—and very real—questions. Why do babies die? Why are there plane crashes? Why do families break up? Why do there have to be such horrible things as heart attacks, cancer, and AIDS? And why are people so violent and evil toward each other?

At 9:02 A.M. on April 19, 1995, a 4800-pound truck bomb exploded in front of the Alfred P. Murrah Federal Building in Oklahoma City, killing 168 innocent people and shocking the entire nation. The evil of terrorism had raised its ugly head in America. Just four days later, one of the greatest advocates for faith in God, Reverend Billy Graham, came to stand up at the memorial service for the Oklahoma City bombing victims and try to make sense out of that horrible tragedy. I watched it on television that day and thought, *What will he say? What can he say?*

Shock and disbelief filled the air. Children had died needlessly. Grandmothers and grandfathers were taken away. Many bodies, hearts, and minds would be bruised for the rest of these people's lives. The hollow emptiness and loneliness which accompanies the loss of loved ones permeated the entire scene. The shock of such an evil act had left our nation stunned.

But as Dr. Graham got up to speak, the mixed tears of grief and hope began to flow. Here, the one person of whom it might rightly be said, "He speaks for God," rose to do his duty. My wife and I wept, too, as we strained to hear every word Dr. Graham would say. When he reached the podium, he told about the questions everyone had asked him: "Why did this happen?" "Why would God have allowed it to happen?"

There was a pause which lasted for what seemed like forever. He then said the three words which disarmed all the critics of the gospel. With a deep and honest sadness in his eyes Graham said, "I don't know."

Like Dr. Graham, we Christians cannot always explain why bad things happen. We simply must accept that for some reason, at certain times, God allows us to walk through a dark valley.

But Dr. Graham did not stop there. We do not have to either. As believers in God, while forced to say, "I don't know to the 'why' of pain," we also have the hopeful joy of being able to say, "But I do know this: When pain comes, because there is a God in heaven who loves us, we do not have to walk through any dark valley alone."

The Suffering God

During World War II, the theologian Dietrich Bonhoeffer was jailed by the Nazis because of his faith. From his prison cell he wrote a note describing where he looked for help. It stated, "Only a suffering God can help." What is that he said? A *suffering* God? How could God suffer? *Why* would God ever have to suffer?

Just a casual look at the life of Jesus will show that He suffered through many of the same painful experiences we suffer in this world. Jesus endured both physical pain and emotional pain. His body was broken for us, and He knew what it was like to be ridiculed by cruel people. He knew what it was like to feel betrayed by a close friend and to lose a loved one to physical death. By entering humanity, Christ personally suffered the same kinds of pain that you and I must endure because of the effects of the Fall.

The Christian answer to suffering and pain is that we serve a suffering God, one who knows what we experience and who has willingly taken upon Himself pain and suffering which were not due to Him. The God of the Bible understands and is able to comfort us because He knows the injustice of pain even better than we do. The pain Jesus experienced was not because of anything He had done, but because of what we had done. He died for *our* sin. God does not ask us to weather a storm that He has not weathered Himself. Dorothy Sayers once said,

> For whatever reason God chose to make man as he is—limited and suffering and subject to sorrows and death—He had the honesty and the courage to take His own medicine. Whatever game He is playing with His creation, He has kept His own rules and played fair. He can exact nothing from man that He has not exacted from Himself. He has Himself gone through the whole of human experience, from the trivial irritations of family life and the cramping restrictions of hard work and lack of money to the worst horrors of pain and humiliation, defeat, despair, and death. When He was a man, He played the man. He was born in poverty and died in disgrace and thought it well worthwhile.[4]

It is in God's plan that one day He will bring suffering to an end. Because Christ was victorious over death, He has dismantled the permanence of death and evil. During our times of pain and suffering, He comforts those who know Him and is calling out to those who do not to come to Him for peace and comfort.

We do not know why we have to endure pain and suffering, but we know we do not have to endure it alone. We do not know exactly what God's purposes are in each case, but we can trust that He knows what we are going through and will turn it into something that works for our ultimate good. William Cowper wrote this poem entitled *God Moves in a Mysterious Way:*

> God moves in mysterious ways
> His wonders to perform;
> He plants His footsteps in the sea,
> And rides upon the storm.
> His purposes will ripen fast,
> Unfolding every hour;
> The bud may have a bitter taste,
> But sweet will be the flower.
> Blind unbelief is sure to err,
> And scan His works in vain:
> God is His own interpreter,
> And He will make it plain.

Possible Reasons Behind Specific Instances of Pain and Suffering

I feel a bit hesitant as I write the next few pages because I do not want anyone reading this to think that I am trivializing their pain and suffering by running through a list of possible reasons for why they might be going through what they are going through. But for the sake of helping make some sense of suffering, I would like to suggest several possible reasons why God allows specific instances of pain and suffering. Perhaps you will see one that applies to your own life.

Pain Can Be a Step Toward a Greater Good

God's primary goal in our lives is to change us. He is intent on developing the character of Christ in all believers. I often cling to the things of this world so tightly that He has to pry my fingers off them so I will more fully place my trust in Him. There can be pain as I resist. There can be fear because I do not always trust that God knows what He is doing. But in the end, all that happens to me is for the greater good of my becoming more like Christ. We must remember that just as in dentistry and surgery, sometimes a little pain can lead to a much greater good.

Pain Can Serve as a Warning Device

Pain can sometimes be an effective warning device. It helps protect us by influencing us to withdraw from harmful activity. Physical pain is primarily associated with injury or the threat of injury to our body. We need pain for our own good. Leprosy is a disease in which the human body loses its ability to feel pain. We might think that sounds like a good idea. But if we cannot feel pain, our body becomes its own worst enemy. If we cannot feel pain, we will not know when we are touching something that will burn our skin or when we have stepped on something that will cut our foot.

Psychological pain, on the other hand, may be a warning to discontinue some activity or attitude in our life. It may be that we are consumed with materialism or popularity and, in the struggle to advance, we experience emotional pain. Sometimes God uses this kind of pain to get our attention and warn us that we have set our affections on the wrong things. As C.S. Lewis has said, "God whispers to us in our pleasures, speaks in our conscience, but shouts in our pains: it is His megaphone to rouse a deaf world." And so pain can be a useful tool God uses to warn us of spiritual danger.

Pain Can Help in Soul-Making

The apostle Paul wrote, "We also exult in our tribulations, knowing that tribulation brings about perseverance; and perseverance, proven character; and proven character, hope; and hope does not disappoint" (Romans 5:3-5). And the apostle James wrote, "Consider it all joy, my brethren, when you encounter various trials, knowing that the testing of your faith produces endurance. And let endurance have its perfect result, so that you may be perfect and complete, lacking in nothing" (James 1:2-4). So we see there is a direct correlation between the tribulations we endure in this life and the work of God in perfecting us and developing mature character in us.

This world is a place where outstanding achievement and terrible disaster can both happen. Only in such a world can real soul-making and character development take place.

Pain Helps Increase Our Sense of Purpose and Mission

There is a sense in which we are the hands, feet, and voice of God. For some reason, God has chosen to use believers as His agents and the ambassadors of His kingdom as one of the means to accomplish His purposes in this world. Because some people experience pain, others then have real opportunities for heroism. When we help people in need, our hearts are enlarged, our lives are enriched, and we begin fulfilling the law of Christ, which is that we should "bear one another's burdens." This in turn inspires other people to do the same, and together we reflect the love and mercy of God by being generous through our giving and other philanthropic endeavors.

If you are in a place of being able to give, become heroic in your giving. If you are in need, be humble enough to let people help, and you will enable them to become more like God.

Storms of Correction and Storms of Perfection

The story of Jonah in the Old Testament[5] is an illustration of how God used pain to correct and discipline someone. God told Jonah to go to Nineveh and preach, but Jonah disobeyed and jumped on a boat headed in the other direction. God sent a storm, and Jonah got thrown overboard. He was swallowed by a great fish and remained alive in its belly for three days. While inside the fish, Jonah repented and prayed for God's deliverance, and God responded. The fish coughed up Jonah, and then Jonah went to Nineveh and preached, and the people repented.

The intense fear, pain, and suffering that Jonah went through was what you might call a storm of correction. God was using pain to correct and discipline His wayward servant.

The story of Jesus' disciples in their boat out on the stormy Sea of Galilee is what might be called a storm of perfection.[6] Jesus was with them in the boat but was asleep. Even though they were professional fishermen, they were frightened by this sudden and violent storm. They cried out to Jesus for help, and He awoke and rebuked the winds and the sea. Immediately it became perfectly calm. Here is an instance of Christ allowing His disciples to go through a time of great fear and anxiety in order to mature their faith and develop their trust in Him as they saw His ability and willingness to respond to their needs.

Pain as Judgment for Specific Sin

There are times when God allows pain as a judgment or punishment for specific sin and rebellion. We saw this with Adam and Eve as they tasted pain, struggle, and death. The story of Jonah is also an example of judgment for his rebellion. In the world, fines and jail sentences act as a deterrent for those who are considering committing crimes. It should be no surprise that God would at times exact punishment from us when we disregard His will in our lives.

But in talking about this, we should take great care, especially when it comes to a discussion of how God may be dealing with any specific case. It is not for any of us to determine when God is or is not meting out punishment for someone else's specific sin. The religious leaders of Jesus' time made the mistake of doing this, and we must learn from their mistake. The only one who has the right to execute judgment and punishment is God Himself. But we should be aware that there are times when God may deal with all of us in this way.

Laws of Nature

Some of the pain that is produced in this world is simply a matter of the normal functioning of the laws of nature. These instances appear gratuitous. When a hurricane rips across Alabama on a Sunday morning and flattens a church where people are worshiping and praying to God, it is very hard to come to terms with what possible good God might have in mind. When earthquakes cause so much death and destruction, it is mind-boggling to even try to figure out why God allows them.

For those of us who have never been victims of these kinds of tragic events, the only meaningful manner in which to view them is to find some way that God wants us to respond to the needs of their victims. This is an opportunity for us to exercise heroism, generosity, self-sacrifice, and compassion.

Special Display of God's Glory

On certain occasions in the Scriptures, pain and suffering have been allowed by God for no other reason than to permit a special opportunity for God to receive glory. One such instance is found in John 9:1-3, where Jesus and His disciples come upon a man who has been blind since birth. The disciples asked Jesus, "Rabbi, who sinned, this man or his parents, that he would be born blind?" Jesus answered by telling the disciples it was neither this man's sin nor his parents' sin, but so that the works of God might be displayed in the blind man's life.

Jesus said the same thing on the occasion of His friend Lazarus's death. When the messengers came with the news of Lazarus being deathly ill, Jesus said, "This sickness is not to end in death, but for the glory of God, so that the Son of God may be glorified by it" (John 11:4).

The miracles of Jesus both confirmed who He was—the promised Christ—and they showed forth His compassion. These are instances when God's glory could be visibly displayed in and through tragic circumstances.

How many times have we heard of situations where people have gone through inconceivable pain or suffering but still showed incredible faith and courage in God and His purposes? Sometimes there is healing and sometimes not, but in the end, their unshakable faith in God is a magnificent testimony that brings glory to God.

As Dorothy Sayers has pointed out, God does not always prevent the expression of evil. Sometimes He transforms it. God did not prevent Judas from betraying Christ, but He turned it into an offer of salvation to the world. God did not stop the crown of thorns from being jammed on the head of Jesus; instead, He turned it into a crown of glory. God did not stop Christ's death on the cross; instead, He turned it into a resurrection day.

Direct Effort of Satan to Defeat or Distract Us

In the heavenly realm, we have an enemy. He is the enemy of our spiritual life in God, the enemy of our marriages, and the enemy of our relationships with our children, our parents, and the church. It is his intention to distract and defeat us as often as he can without being spotted in the process. The apostle Peter reminds us:

> Be of sober spirit, be on the alert. Your adversary, the devil, prowls about like a roaring lion, seeking someone to devour. But resist him, firm in your faith, knowing that the same experiences of suffering are being accomplished by your brethren who are in the world. And after you have suffered for a little while, the God of all grace, who called you to His eternal glory in Christ, will Himself perfect, confirm, strengthen and establish you (1 Peter 5:8-10).

As in the case with Job, there are times when the devil and his minions are allowed to come after us. God knows when that is happening, and God is always in charge. We need not fear the devil, for he has already been defeated by the power of Christ's death and resurrection. But misery loves company, and so the devil does what he can to sidetrack those who have fixed their hope on Christ. That is why Peter said we should be sober of spirit and on the alert.

Understanding Pain

In the story *The Velveteen Rabbit,* all the toys in the nursery wanted to be real. As a relative newcomer, the Velveteen Rabbit was not sure what it meant to be real, so he decided to ask the Skin Horse, who had been around for quite some time and who seemed very wise.

> "What is real?" asked the Rabbit one day, when they were lying side by side in the nursery. "Does it mean having things that buzz inside you and a stick-out handle?"
>
> "Real isn't how you are made," said the Skin Horse. "It is a thing that happens to you. When a child loves you for a long, long time, not just to play with, but REALLY loves you, then you become Real."
>
> "Does it hurt?" asked the Rabbit.
>
> "Sometimes," said the Skin Horse, for he was always truthful. "When you are Real, you do not mind being hurt."
>
> "Does it happen all at once, like being wound up," he asked, "or bit by bit?"
>
> "It doesn't happen all at once," said the Skin Horse. "You become. It takes a long time. That's why it doesn't often happen to people who break easily, or have sharp edges, or who have to be carefully kept. Generally, by the time you are Real, most of your hair has been loved off, and your eyes drop out and you get loose in the joints and very shabby. But these things do not matter at all, because once you are Real you can't be ugly, except to people who do not understand" (Margery Williams, *The Velveteen Rabbit*).

Your life and mine are significant simply because we are loved by God. He is in the business of making us real by loving us.

The way we react to pain and suffering will determine whether life's most tragic experiences bring us bitterness and despair or opportunities for growth and blessing. As Dorothy Sayers has written:

> Christianity has an enormous advantage over every other religion in the world. It is the *only* religion which gives value to evil and suffering. It affirms—not, like Christian Science, that evil has no real existence, nor yet, like Buddhism, that good consists in a refusal to experience evil—but that perfection is attained through the active and positive effort to wrench a real good out of a real evil.[7]

Whatever pain or suffering you may be experiencing or have experienced, you can trust that God, in His divine purposes, has allowed it for your greatest good. He does not ask you to understand it fully; you only need to trust Him in the same way that someone might expect earthly children to trust their loving parents. And as we place our confidence in God, trusting Him fully, the peace of God which goes beyond our comprehension is promised to be ours and we, like the Velveteen Rabbit, take another step closer to becoming real.

- *Has God forgiven us for everything we have done, no matter how bad?*
- *Is all guilt bad?*
- *What can I do to free myself from this overwhelming sense of guilt?*
- *How can I experience God's forgiveness in my life?*

12

Receiving: How Can I Experience God's Forgiveness?

Forgiveness is man's deepest need and highest achievement.

HORACE BUSHNELL

My mom works at the Pentagon. I cannot tell you much about the specifics of her job (for your own safety, of course), but let's just say she is involved in the military.

Early one evening, the phone in Mom's office rang when she happened to be there to pick it up. The voice on the other end was that of an older man, who said he did not know whether she was the right person to ask, but that he was interested in finding out whether the military had kept records of certain incidents that occurred during World War II. "Which certain incidents?" Mom asked. The gentleman cleared his throat, mumbled a little, and then told her what had happened.

He was a veteran and had been stationed in France during the war. One night he and several buddies left their base and headed for a bar in the nearby village. After several hours and far too much alcohol, they started back to the base. Along the way, they picked a fight with a man from the village and literally beat the poor fellow to a pulp. The victim hardly put up a fight. They left him by the side of the road, not even sure he was still breathing.

Later that night, back at the base, MPs came through their barracks, trying to find out who had done this. He and his friends stood in statue-like silence, afraid of getting found out. For more than 50 years, this man had lived with the burden of guilt for his unconscionable act.

The caller went on to tell my mom that recently he had become a Christian, and after all those years he felt that God wanted him to find the man and set things right. It is likely the man had had some expensive medical bills as a result of his injuries, and the caller wanted to make restitution.

My mom is the perfect person to have received this man's call. She has had a lot of experience saying things like, "Don't you worry. God can take care of this. He loves you so much." God knows my mom's heart. She has seen both sides of forgiveness, and He directed this man's call straight to her desk.

Mom told the man that, unfortunately, there were no records like the ones he was looking for. During a war it is impossible to document everything, and in addition, some records are blown up, burned up, or otherwise destroyed during fighting. She then added that, by God's providence, his call had come to her, and that she, too, was a Christian. That being said, she encouraged him to acknowledge God's full forgiveness. He had done all he could. He had been sensitive to the conviction of the Holy Spirit. He had been willing to make things right, even though it might have cost him something. God had brought him to the place where his heart was soft again, the ears of his conscience healthy and hearing again. He was truly sorry and had honestly admitted his guilt. In becoming a Christian, he had allowed God the joy of setting him free and wiping the slate clean, and now it was time to simply receive the assurance of God's forgiveness.

With a tearful stammer, the grateful old veteran thanked Mom and said good-bye, the burden lifted, the stain of his sin washed away. He had been humbled by experiencing the great forgiveness of God.

The Quiet Voice of Conscience

Someone has said, "Confession is good for the soul, but bad for the reputation." But what happens when the individuals of a culture become concerned about their reputation to the exclusion of their soul? Can any of us afford to prefer our reputation over our soul?

John Wooden, the former UCLA basketball coach, once said, "Be more concerned with your character than with your reputation, because your character is what you really are, while your reputation is merely what others think you are." We live in a culture that trivializes substance and worships celebrity. We are obsessed with image and appearances. Yet it is the soul that is the seat of character and conscience. Conscience is the means through which God speaks to call us to Himself, to convince us of what is true, to remind us of what is right and what is wrong.

Back during the war, the caller who spoke to my mom had learned to ignore his conscience. No longer stirred by its uneasiness, he was capable of great evil. Later, after he became a Christian, the Holy Spirit renewed the sensitivity of his conscience and then went on to lead the man to seek restoration. God sent him to my mom, one of God's agents of compassion, and she spoke the gracious words that confirmed God's forgiveness.

Wise King Solomon once said, "He who conceals his transgressions will not prosper, but he who confesses and forsakes them will find compassion" (Proverbs 28:13). That is so true. When our conscience is healthy, God uses it to flag us down, warning us of error and making us aware of our true guilt when we have done wrong. A healthy conscience is the relentless, haunting voice of God's Spirit in our lives. As Mark Twain quipped, "An uneasy conscience is a hair in the mouth." That is precisely what God designed it to be: the persistent, sometimes annoying reminder that we are headed down the wrong road.

Fortunately, in His mercy God does not leave us without hope. When we sin, we put distance between ourselves and the Lord. But God is in the business of restoration. When we confess and turn away from our sin, God restores us in His love and compassion. The road back may seem long, tedious, and sometimes costly, but as Max Lucado has said, "If there are a thousand steps between us and God, He will take all but one."

The Road to Restoration

You have probably heard the story of another person who was humbled by God's great forgiveness. In Luke 15, Jesus tells the parable of a prodigal son who was full of youthful pride and greed. He had an insatiable lust for autonomy. In his self-centered naïveté, he thought he did not need his father, family, or anyone else. He demanded his share of the inheritance and left his family behind.

He headed off to a faraway land, with big plans to live it up and enjoy all that life had to offer him. But after a while, the young man ran out of money. As his fortune dissolved, so did his deluded confidence. Finally, he ended up working on a pig farm, feeding hogs, poverty-stricken. Desperately hungry, he wished he could steal some of the pigs' food.

Jesus tells us that one day the prodigal came to his senses. He recognized his foolishness and determined to head for home, planning to confess his sin and seek his father's mercy. He would try to convince his father to give him a job as a hired servant.

As he approached his family home, a surprising thing happened. From a distance, his father saw him coming. He ran out to meet his wayward son, thrilled to see him again, and he embraced him and kissed him.

Immediately the son began to confess his sinfulness, but the father said nothing. It was as if the father already knew how his son felt. Displaying an amazing grace, the father did not give one hint of "I told you so." Rather, he put a ring on his son's finger, called for a fine robe to be brought, and ordered up some roast beef to throw a welcome-home party. In short, he fully restored his son with joy and gladness.

What a tremendous illustration of both the mercy and grace of God. The prodigal son did not get what he did deserve (rejection), and he did get something he did not deserve (restoration). Matthew Henry makes this insightful comment: "The prodigal came home between hope and fear, fear of being rejected and hope of being received; but his father was not only better to him than his fears, but better to him than his hopes." This is the way it is with our heavenly Father as well. We are all like the prodigal. We have all demanded our own way. We have all taken what the Father has freely given us and wasted it. We have all craved autonomy and unbridled pleasure and have left Him out of our lives.

But just like the prodigal, we have been offered a road to restoration with God. Once we recognize we have distanced ourselves from God, when we find ourselves out of our own resources, when we are lying facedown in the mud of some faraway land, keenly aware of our bankruptcy and brokenness, then the Father reveals our road back home. Our way back to Him includes five simple elements.

Acknowledging Our Sin

First, like the prodigal, we need to *acknowledge our sin.* Like they say in the South, we need to "'fess up," which means we must own up to the fact that we are in the wrong. Humans have perfected the art of blame-shifting. It started right after the very first sin was committed, when God asked Adam and Eve about what they had done. Adam's first words were, "The woman you gave me..." Then God asked Eve the same question, and her first words were, "The serpent..." Adam blamed Eve, Eve blamed the serpent, but nobody "'fessed up."

Ever since the time of Adam and Eve, whenever possible, we have played dodgeball with our deserved blame and true guilt. We live in a false paradise of self-deluded innocence.[1] As Brennan Manning observed of the human race, "In a world where the only plea is 'Not guilty,' what possibility is there for an honest encounter with Jesus, who died for our sins? We can only *pretend* that we are sinners, and thus only *pretend* that we are forgiven."[2]

Now, as Christians, we must realize how counterproductive this is to receiving God's forgiveness. Forgiveness does not apply to faultless "mistakes" or things that happen "to us." Forgiveness is possible only when there has been an infraction, a breaking of some trust, a real offense. Sin is rebellion against God and the distortion of what He has called good. Sin is something we choose to do. It is willful disobedience. Masking it, renaming it, calling it a genetic quirk, an "unfortunate choice," an "illness," blaming it on our environment, our dysfunctional family, or anything else, does us no good whatsoever. We need to ask God to supply us with the moral courage to come clean and deal with our sin head-on. Unless we acknowledge our real sin, we cannot experience real forgiveness.

If our conscience is healthy and is working as God designed it to, our sin will weigh us down. And in spite of what the preachers of pop psychology might say, I believe this is good, because our conscience is telling us the truth. God's answer for sin and guilt is not blame-shifting or denial, it is forgiveness. C.S. Lewis understood this when he said, "What we call asking God's forgiveness very often really consists in asking God to accept our excuses.... What we have got to take to him is the inexcusable bit, the sin."[3] When we go before God, we must leave our excuses behind. We must "'fess up" and acknowledge our sin.

Turning Away from Our Sin

Once we acknowledge our sin, the second element that moves us toward restoration can come into play, which is that we need to repent, or *turn away from our sin.*

What is repentance? The original Greek word is *metanoia,* and it means "a change of mind that institutes a change in life." Repentance means turning around. And when you are on the wrong road, that is exactly what you must do. If you are ever to make any real progress, you must turn around and go back to the right road, and begin heading in the right direction again. Turning away from sin means getting back to thinking as God does about what is right and wrong.

Repentance is not a mere exercise in thinking. It is not just academic or emotional assent to the fact we have sinned. Repentance is doing something about what we say we believe. It implies that we have a choice and can take some action. It means we are not predetermined or preprogrammed to mess up by our environment, temptations, or genetics. There is dignity in repentance, in that it serves to remind us that our moral life is above fatalistic acquiescence. The apostle Paul confirms this: "No temptation has overtaken you but such as is common to man; and God is faithful, who will not allow you to be tempted beyond what you are able, but with the temptation will provide the way of escape also, so that you will be able to endure it" (1 Corinthians 10:13).

Confessing Our Sin

Next we need to make a *genuine confession of our sin.* Have you ever had anyone apologize to you, and after he did, you still were not sure he really meant it? Maybe he stated his apology like this: "I'm sorry *if* I offended you." That *if* sure can change the way on apology comes off. Perhaps we would all do better if we agreed that a genuine apology can never be stated with the word *if* in it.

A genuine confession involves admitting that real wrong was done. It means we clearly understand that we have offended the other person and caused him or her inconvenience, loss, or pain. But every sin we commit is also an offense against God. Though the action we took may have directly hurt our mother, father, brother, or sister, we have also offended our holy God by mistreating those people. Our sins are not just on the "horizontal plane." They are all "vertical" as well. When we sin, we need to go to God with a genuine confession and apology for our sins so that we can experience His forgiveness.

Some of us struggle with chronic temptation toward a specific sin and find ourselves confessing the same sin many times, over and over again. This may cause us to become hopeless or despairing over our repeated failures. Cornelius Plantinga compares confession of sin to a routine household chore: "Recalling and confessing our sin is like taking out the garbage: once is not enough." There are many people who wrestle with a certain sin and find themselves taking out the same garbage over and over again. But we should not lose confidence in God's declaration that we are forgiven, since it is Jesus Himself "in whom we have redemption, the forgiveness of sins" (Colossians 1:14).

Forgiveness for Our Sin

If our journey down the road to restoration is to continue, we will need to realize that God has offered us *real forgiveness.* Humans are not good at this. We tend to bury the hatchet with the handle sticking out of the ground so we will be able to find it and take it up again should the need arise. But God's forgiveness has buried both hatchet and handle. As Martin Luther King Jr. said, "Forgiveness is not an occasional act; it is a permanent attitude." Forgiveness is the permanent attitude of God and the standing promise of the Bible for all those who place their faith in Christ.

This is where Christian spirituality has infinitely more substance than the new spiritualities. Fate cannot forgive. An energy force cannot forgive. Only a God with a face, a personal God, can forgive. Before the God who will one day judge us all, the forgiveness of our sins was purchased by Christ once and for all when He died on the cross in our place. Jesus Christ paid the debt that we owed to God, and now, through Christ, we have real forgiveness, the only way to permanently deal with guilt and sin. And this brings me to the final step on the road to restoration.

Receiving God's Forgiveness

With grateful hearts and in true humility, we must *receive the forgiveness offered* by the grace of God. Here is how restoration becomes complete. On our end of things, God's forgiveness is not achieved; it is simply received. Its power is not dependent on the one who has been forgiven, but on the One who did the forgiving. As my wife, Kim, has said in her book *Simplicity: Finding Peace by Uncluttering Your Life,*

> The truth is that our forgivability is not the issue. The issue is *who* the Forgiver is. At my very best, I am not deserving. William Langland said, "And all the wickedness in the world that man might work or think is no more to the mercy of God than a live coal in the sea."[4]

Our complete forgiveness was purchased by Christ's death on the cross. Once we have confessed our sin, we must refocus our attention from ourselves and our sin onto Christ, remembering what He achieved for us through His death. The Bible teaches that "in Him we have redemption through His blood, the forgiveness of our trespasses, according to the riches of His grace" (Ephesians 1:7). We have been cleansed by the blood of Christ, which simply means that in the spiritual realm, before God, the slate has been wiped clean. And because of this, like the prodigal son's father, God welcomes us home with a full embrace, with joy and gladness!

Perhaps you are wrestling with something you have done that you know was wrong. Maybe you have a chronic problem with temptation, and you think God has grown tired of forgiving you. We may try to lock our secret sins in a closet and throw away the key, hoping no one will find them out. But the problem is still on our own conscience. God knows about it, too. Even the devil knows about it, and he will use that knowledge to accuse, immobilize, and demoralize us. Unless we unlock and open up the closet door, acknowledging our sin and brokenness, unless we admit we are not perfect, and that we struggle with things like pride, arrogance, anger, bitterness, and lust, we will never be able to move down the road to restoration and freedom.

Let me encourage you to seize this opportunity to be set free from the guilt and pollution your sinfulness may be causing your soul. Acknowledge your sin, repent from it, and confess your sins to God. He will not be shocked by anything you have done. Over the course of human history, He has seen much worse, many times. God is not pleased that you and I sin, but He is thrilled when everything His Son achieved on the cross becomes effective in our lives.

Christian spirituality offers a unique answer to the problem of true guilt. It is a truly clear conscience brought about by real forgiveness through Christ. "If we confess our sins, He is faithful and righteous to forgive us our sins and to cleanse us from all unrighteousness" (1 John 1:9).

- *What does God want us to become?*
- *Does God want the same thing for everyone?*
- *Why are we alive?*
- *What does spiritual growth look like?*

13

Becoming: What Does It Take to Grow Spiritually?

Grace is never a stationary thing, it is always found in a becoming.

MEISTER ECKHART

When I was a little kid, I just could not wait to grow up. I looked forward to the days when I would be just like the "big" people. I wanted to drive a car, get married, have a checking account, and not have to clean my plate at every meal. There was something exciting about growing up. Even though I knew it did not happen all at once, I looked forward to getting the process started.

Christian spirituality also involves a desire to grow up. The Christian journey is a life in motion because it is always a life of growth. This is no static spirituality! In a word, Christian spirituality is a "becoming."

It all starts when we become a Christian by accepting Christ as our Lord and Savior. At that time, God deals with the legal problem of our sin by wiping the slate clean. God forgives us for our sin based on the things done by Christ, who died on the cross in our place. The Bible calls this *justification by faith,* and it is the one-time, once-and-for-all work of Christ on our behalf. But then our spiritual growth continues as the Holy Spirit transforms our daily lives and gives us power over temptation and sin. This day-to-day working out of our salvation is an ongoing process that the Bible calls *sanctification*, which means "to set apart," or "to make holy." As God changes our hearts, step-by-step and bit by bit, we see the fruit of the Spirit is work in our life.

Francis Schaeffer expressed it this way: "But after we become Christians, the moments proceed, the clock continues to tick; and in every moment of time, our calling is to believe God, raise the empty hands of faith, and let fruit flow out through us." In raising the empty hands of faith, we humbly recognize that it is God who is at work in us, both to will and to work for His good pleasure. God provides the power; our part is to turn to Him and receive what He offers.

But we must not make the mistake of thinking we are passive in our spiritual growth. Our faith requires nurture and maintenance on our part. It is not just the acknowledgment of correct doctrine. A growing faith is built upon the foundation of God's Word, empowered by the Holy Spirit, and then put into practice as a matter of the will and disposition. As Christian ethicist David Clyde Jones has said, "The real problem of ethics is not in finding the rule to direct us how to glorify and enjoy God but in having the will to make this our aim in the first place." Are we aiming at spiritual growth? Do we truly desire to glorify and enjoy God?

This principle of the involvement of the will is seen in a wonderful old poem:

> One ship drives east and another drives west
> With the selfsame winds that blow;
> 'Tis the set of the sails
> And not the gales
> Which tells us the way to go.
>
> —Ella Wheeler Wilcox

So, let me ask you: In which direction are your spiritual sails set? Setting our sails means living intentionally, fixing our course. If we are to grow spiritually, a couple of things will be required from us. First, the direction of a sailing ship is controlled by the rudder as it turns in one direction or another. You can turn a ship in such a direction that will allow it to catch the wind in its sails, you can try to sail against the wind, or you can simply tie up the sails and lie adrift.

Turning the ship of our lives into the wind of God's Spirit means putting ourselves in the path of God's grace. This includes carving out time to fill our hearts and minds with the Word of God and to commune with God in prayer, confessing our sins and receiving God's forgiveness daily. It includes making time for worshiping God, serving God and others, and being with God's people. Through these and other spiritual disciplines, the life of the spirit is nurtured and encouraged to grow.

These are not once-for-all efforts. We do not just accept Christ and then forget about it. We need to commit ourselves to practicing the spiritual disciplines on a regular basis. We need to be filled and refilled with the Spirit over and over again because, frankly, we leak. But God is rich in grace, and His mercies are new every morning. Our daily prayer can be, "Lord, fill me with Your Spirit once again." God provides the power for motion. We turn into the wind of the Spirit, and He fills us, enabling us to follow where He leads us.

The Desire to Want What God Wants

I live in Nashville, Tennessee, also known as "Music City, USA." In addition to being the home of country music, this town is also considered the hub of activity for contemporary Christian music. As you might imagine, there are a lot of Christians who are songwriters and musicians who have come to Nashville. Some of them moved here because they thought God wanted them to. They believed that God had gifted them and was going to use their musical endeavors somehow, so they headed off to the place that seems to be the center for that kind of activity.

There are also a few people who moved here because they thought God told them He was going to make them big-time recording stars. It is not that they run around saying it out loud all the time. It is more latent. Yet somehow they believe they have heard a spiritual calling to become a "Christian" version of a superstar celebrity, complete with all the fame and fortune the Christian music business has to offer.

This reminds me of the times I used to say jokingly that I thought God was calling me to start a ministry in some exotic vacation spot like Hawaii or the south of France. I have tried to find examples of those kinds of ministry callings in Scripture to justify what I wanted to do, but I have not been able to find any yet. (If you know where they are, please do let me know so I can get on with my calling and start a church on Maui or the French Riviera.)

My point is, there are people who seem to equate the ideas in their own head with the voice of God. I am not saying there is anything wrong with wanting to pursue the dreams you have or the vocations you may be wanting to try out. That is not my point at all. But we should be honest enough not to confuse our personal ambitions with God's will. Sometimes they will be in line with each other, and sometimes they will not.

Am I saying that when people pursue their own ambitions, they have misread God? Sometimes. Am I suggesting that people are completely incapable of hearing from God? No. Are we doomed to wander around in a fog about what God's will is for our lives? Not at all. But when we pray for God to reveal His will for our lives, we need to make sure we are not really just asking Him to show us how to make more money, advance in our career, find a new boyfriend, or obtain the things *we* think will make our life more convenient, comfortable, entertaining, and fun. In regard to this, F.B. Meyer wrote, "So long as there is some thought of personal advantage, some idea of acquiring the praise and commendation of men, some aim of self-aggrandizement, it will be simply impossible to find out God's purpose concerning us."[1]

That said, we must admit that we will always have some mixture of right and wrong motives. But we are still responsible to ask the question, "Do I want what God wants for my life?" It is important to prayerfully check our motives when we are trying to discern God's will. Jesus gave us a guiding principle that will help: "If anyone wishes to come after Me, he must deny himself, and take up his cross and follow Me. For whoever wishes to save his life will lose it; but whoever loses his life for My sake will find it" (Matthew 16:24-25). There is a kind of ambition here. It is the ambition to follow Jesus and to "save" our life. But it is clearly not a self-centered ambition. It is an ambition filled with abandonment and allegiance: abandonment of selfishness and allegiance to Christ. It is the laying down of our life in surrender so that we want what God wants.

Three Things We Should Want

In the Lord's prayer we pray, "Hallowed be Your name. Your kingdom come. Your will be done, on earth as it is in heaven" (Matthew 6:9-10). If we desire to be led by the Spirit, we must find ourselves wanting three things. We must be devoted to "hallowing" His name, which simply means regarding His name and His person as sacred. Instead of distorting or denigrating the name of God by the way we live, we make it our purpose to live in such a way as to honor the name of God. We must also be committed to advancing His kingdom, which is not so much a geographic kingdom as it is the reign of God in the lives of His people. It includes the idea of an ever-increasing submission to His lordship. And third, we must devote our lives to seeing His will done here on earth just as it is in heaven. This necessarily includes seeing that God's will is done in our own lives.

Anything but Dull

The apostle Paul, in a broad and sweeping statement, tells us something else about those who are being led by the Spirit: "All who are being led by the Spirit of God, these are sons of God" (Romans 8:14). This is evidence of our adoption as children of God. We find ourselves wanting, desiring, longing to be led by the Holy Spirit as we set ourselves to do the will of our Father in each immediate moment. Picking up dry cleaning, going to the post office, raking leaves, chauffeuring our children, and interacting in relationships with everyone from our spouse to the community at large, we have the opportunity to be led by the Spirit.

Notice the word is *led*. The Holy Spirit leads by persuasion, not by coercion. There is no force involved. True believers are led by the Spirit and follow joyfully because they delight in doing God's will.

I have two miniature schnauzers, a salt-and-pepper-colored one named Rose and a black one named Violet. When I walk them on the leash, they pull as hard as they can, stretching the leash for all the length they can get out of it. If I were to let go of the leash, they would be gone in a flash.

Rose and Violet do not know any better, but they remind me of the many people who call themselves Christians yet who will ask, "Can I do such-and-such a thing and still be a Christian?" Well, because we are saved by grace and not by what we do, the answer is technically yes. Christ died for our sins, and He died for all of them, no matter how "big" or "small" we might think they are. But, setting aside the question about any individual act of sin, doesn't it seem strange that someone who says he truly desires to follow Christ would even be asking how far out on the edge he can go, or how far he can stretch the leash and still be considered a Christian? What does that say about his spiritual disposition?

Jesus said, "I came that they may have life, and have it abundantly" (John 10:10). As we begin to want what God wants in our lives, life becomes increasingly full of surprises. It becomes the greatest of great adventures, and we are constantly refilled with astonishment and wonder. God is behind the steering wheel, and we never know precisely which way He will turn us. This is what makes the Christian faith anything but dull. Wanting what God wants requires a certain kind of reckless abandon, a passionate allegiance, and a ferocious trust.

What God Wants

So what exactly does God want? How can we know what God's goal is for our lives? The answers to those questions will help us identify when it is God who is speaking, leading, and guiding us. God wouldn't lead us into something that runs against His goal for our lives. If we are curious about whether we should do something or not, we can test the ideas we are considering to see whether they move us deeper into what God wants.

In identifying what God wants, we should distinguish between the *general* will of God and the *particular* will of God. The general will of God includes that which has been revealed for all people, at all times, everywhere. This includes what we refer to as the Ten Commandments, and it includes Jesus' summary of God's law:

> "You shall love the LORD your God with all your heart, and with all your soul, and with all your mind." This is the great and foremost commandment. The second is like it, "You shall love your neighbor as yourself." On these two commandments depend the whole Law and the Prophets (Matthew 22:37-40).

These things are what God wants from all people, at all times, everywhere.

The particular will of God deals with things such as our jobs, whether or whom we should marry, where we live, and so on. I will not pretend to give you an answer to questions about God's particular will for your life. That must come from the Lord to you. You must set yourself to hear His voice as He speaks through the various means He chooses. But I would like to emphasize that the general outlines of God's will have been revealed in Scripture, and they can often help us answer any specific questions we are wrestling with. We must commit ourselves to the *general* will of God if we want to know and be guided by the *particular* will of God. Then we can allow what is clear to help us interpret what is not yet clear.

In the record of God's creation of human beings, we are given a glimpse of what God's primary goal is for all of our lives. In Genesis 1:26-27 we are told:

> God said, "Let Us make man in Our image, according to Our likeness; and let them rule over the fish of the sea and over the birds of the sky and over the cattle and over all the earth, and over every creeping thing that creeps on the

> earth." God created man in His own image, in the image of God He created him; male and female He created them.

Did you notice the repeated theme, that human beings were intentionally created in the image of God? This reveals the primary goal God has for our lives. It is not about wealth or poverty, career advancement or loss of a job. It is not about academic achievement or social improvement. God wants His image to be reflected in us. What an awesome privilege! What an honor! The infinite God of all creation carefully designed each one of us to reflect His image!

Some of you might be thinking that this sounds a little odd. You look in the mirror and it makes you wonder why in the world God would want His image to be reflected in you. Why not the Grand Canyon, the Mediterranean, or the Milky Way? What about the eagle, the lion, or the antelope? Those things are awesome, beautiful, and inspiring to everyone. Why would God want to reflect His image in a plumber from South Dakota, a taxi-mom from Phoenix, or a social worker from the Bronx?

The reason is quite simple. It is because this is not about what you look like or what you do. This is about the potential God sees in you simply because of who He made you to be and who He wants you to become.

Why You Are Alive

Christian spirituality is like a detective story, but as G.K. Chesterton says, it is a *divine* detective story. It is not so much concerned with why a person is dead, but why he or she is alive. Here is the secret that philosophers have been trying to search out for a long, long time—the one they call the *summum bonum,* or the highest good. It is the most noble pursuit, the key to fulfillment and satisfaction in life. The highest good for your life and mine is that God's image would be reflected in us.

People often ask, "What's the meaning of life? Why are we alive? Do our lives have any real purpose?" The Bible answers these questions by telling us that yes, we do have a purpose, and it goes far beyond punching a time card, far beyond the mundane routine of family responsibilities, far beyond our obsessions with appearance, fitness, or the approval of other people. It goes far beyond the things we own and far beyond all the thrills our money can buy. The purpose of life is that we would reflect God's image! God did not plan that for any other part of creation. All of creation declares God's glory, but only human beings reflect God's image. What a joyful opportunity we have to live extraordinary lives! Each moment of each day is pregnant with possibilities for us to reflect the image of God wherever we go, whatever we do.

The trip to the grocery store is no longer just to get milk, soup, and cereal. We can reflect God's image as we pull into the parking lot, as we go up and down each aisle, and even waiting in line at the checkout behind that lady with all the coupons. Answering the phone becomes an adventure of seeing how God might cause His image to be reflected through us to the person calling. Going to church is no longer about what we can get out of the worship service, but about what we can bring to it as we seek to reflect God's image to those we meet there.

Once we begin to want what God wants for our lives, then we can begin learning how to become the person He wants us to become.

Becoming God's Person

A well-known young actress was once asked her opinion on smoking cigarettes. She replied, "Smoking kills. If you're killed, you've lost a very important part of your life."

Mmmmm. I suppose that is true. There are some views of spirituality that promote the loss of another very important part of your life. They suggest that the goal of spirituality is the assimilation of your personality into the great cosmic unity, which of course requires the loss of your personality. The more spiritual you become, the more *you* disappear.

Pardon the simpleness of my question, but why would you even want to get out of bed, much less go about your daily life, if you were destined to disappear? Where is the hope for meaning in a spirituality whose primary goal is that you cease to exist and are fused into some divine version of *Star Trek*'s "Borg"?

This idea is the complete opposite of that found in Christian spirituality. The Christian faith teaches that our personalities are unique, that we have real value and purpose, and that the goal of our spiritual life is not assimilation. When Christians grow spiritually, they become more and more the one-of-a-kind people God has created them to be. We are not supposed to become mindless clones of anyone else. God created us as rational, self-aware individuals who live in dynamic relationship with our rational, self-aware Creator and with other rational, self-aware individuals.

Christian spirituality teaches that our personalities are destined for distinction, not extinction. Each of us is an original, uniquely created by God for His glory, and designed to remain that way for eternity. Nor do our personalities disappear when we die a physical death. When Jesus was on the Mount of Transfiguration, Peter, James, and John saw Him talking with two identifiable individuals who had long since died physically: Moses and Elijah. If human personality fades to nothingness when we die, Jesus would not have been talking with two persons who had names.

In the New Testament Book of Hebrews, we read about some of the giants of the faith—men and women whose stories are told throughout the Scriptures, but who died a long time ago. The author goes on to paint a word picture of those of us who are still alive on earth, describing us as if we were running the race of faith in an athletic stadium. The stands are filled with the saints who have already finished their race. They are called a "great cloud of witnesses." Though they have died physically, they still exist as distinct personalities, and because of Christ's resurrection victory over death, we will all one day rise to live with the Lord and with each other forever.

According to the Bible, while we are alive and here on earth we are supposed to be growing spiritually, becoming more and more like Christ in our character. And when you think about it, Jesus was the most fully human person to ever live. As we become more like Christ, we become more fully human, too, doing what humans were originally designed to do: reflect God's image. We draw closer and closer to the Lord, not in hopes of being absorbed or assimilated, but to more accurately reflect His image by more fully becoming the person He wants us to be.

Avoiding the False Yous

The *Brookesia perarmata,* otherwise known as a chameleon, looks like some kind of monster from a little child's worst nightmare. It has horns, a dorsal crest, a long and fast tongue to catch its prey, and eyes that operate independently, rotating like machine-gun turrets, which allows it to see in two directions at once.

Chameleons are best known for their ability to change color. But what most people do not know is that when chameleons do change color, it is not only to match their background. They may change color because of their health or body temperature, to attract another chameleon, or to hide from a predator. And most chameleons have what is called a "rest coloration"—that is, a color they revert to that is their true self.

There were times I lived my life like a human chameleon, eyes shifting, looking around in every direction, trying to see what everybody else was doing so I could adjust and fit in, and not be left out or thought poorly of. Over the years, I got pretty good at it and could change color based on whatever group I was with at the moment. I could turn on a dime to fit in with whomever I was with. But what I have discovered is, when you live your life as a social chameleon, you never have a sense of just being yourself.

I am not saying there is anything wrong with wanting to be loved or liked. But speaking from my own experience, if we are always adjusting ourselves to win the approval of other people or to hide our true selves from others, we will find ourselves either disappearing into a fog of schizophrenia or drowning in an ocean of anxiety.

God created each of us to be our unique selves, and when we focus on becoming the individuals God designed us to be, we begin to find our "rest coloration." And take it from a recovering chameleon like me, the rest is more than worth the risk.

Christian spirituality includes the call for you and me to turn away from all the false selves we might be tempted to try to become out of envy, curiosity, insecurity, or greed. God's will is never for us to become something or someone we are not. He has created each of us with a special combination of gifts, talents, and abilities that can be employed in His service and that will bring glory to His name.

Do not waste time and energy trying to be somebody else. If you do that, you will stop being *you.* And if you are not being you, you can bet nobody else will be. When God created you, He had someone special in mind who could reflect His image in a unique way. If you do not become the person God wants you to be, the spot God created for you to fill will remain empty. In other words, be yourself. We all need you, and God wants you! Personal authenticity is a high act of worship.

We are not all the same. As a matter of fact, some of us are *very* different. My wife is perhaps the most distinctly different individual I have ever known, and she has a very unusual combination of gifts and talents. She is a highly disciplined, well-organized person, but she is also very creative. She is an author, a musician, a poet, and a painter, but she can also do the taxes! I marvel at her sometimes. It could only be an infinitely creative God who could have designed a person like Kim. She is being conformed to the likeness of Christ as she is faithful to living out who she was uniquely designed to be. And each of us can be conformed to Him in the same way.

Discovering Your Spiritual Gifts

If you have never done it, you should prayerfully identify the spiritual gifts God has given you so you can put them to use and become more the person He made you to be. In Romans the apostle Paul identifies some of the gifts God gives us and offers us instruction in the attitude with which we are to put them to work:

> Since we have gifts that differ according to the grace given to us, each of us is to exercise them accordingly: if prophecy, according to the proportion of his faith; if service, in his serving; or he who teaches, in his teaching; or he who exhorts, in his exhortation; he who gives, with liberality; he who leads, with diligence; he who shows mercy, with cheerfulness. Let love be without hypocrisy. Abhor what is evil; cling to what is good. Be devoted to one another in brotherly love; give preference to one another in honor; not lagging behind in diligence, fervent in spirit, serving the Lord; rejoicing in hope, persevering in tribulation, devoted to prayer, contributing to the needs of the saints, practicing hospitality (Romans 12:6-13).

Here is a pretty clear example of God's will for our lives. There is enough there to keep us busy for quite some time. Do you find yourself wanting to bring home every stray dog? Maybe you have the gift of mercy. Do you find yourself questioning the message behind every movie or TV show? Perhaps you have the gift of teaching. Do you find yourself inviting people to your house for dinner all the time? Perhaps you have the gift of hospitality. Look for yourself in this list, and ask God to show you how and where He might like you to start using your spiritual gifts.

I look at this passage and immediately find myself challenged by the humility and selfless devotion to which we are called as we put the gifts God has given us into action. Christ wants each of us to use our gifts for a purpose higher than our own self-interests. We're supposed to use these gifts to glorify God and serve our brothers and sisters. That is part of giving your life away and then finding it again.

Being Transformed

I'm usually so obsessed with my own wants and needs that I fail to focus my life on God's will or the good of other people. Paul anticipates this when he tells us,

> Do not be conformed to this world, but be transformed by the renewing of your mind, so that you may prove what the will of God is, that which is good and acceptable and perfect (Romans 12:2).

This world says, "Look out for yourself. Take care of good ol' number one. Climb the ladder of success, and if you have to step on a few people in the process, so be it!" But God does not want us to conform to that message. As Richard Foster says,

> The fruit of the Spirit is not push, drive, climb, grasp, and trample. Do not let the rat-racing world keep you on its treadmill. There is a legitimate place for blood, sweat, and tears; but it should have its roots in the call of God, not in the desire to get ahead. Life is more than a climb to the top of the heap.[2]

That climb to the top takes a lot out of a human personality. It requires so many compromises and results in so many needless casualties. The money you make, the power you gain, the pleasure you find—these pursuits may be fine in the right context, but an obsession with them is sure to callous your soul. As comedienne Lily Tomlin put it, "The trouble with the rat race is, even if you win, you're still a rat."

I do not mean to offend you if you happen to like rats, but the truth is, rats were not created in the image of God. Paul says human beings have an opportunity to "prove what the will of God is" as His image is reflected in our transformed minds and lives. If you have been living the life of a rat, I want you to know that God has the power to change you. As you yield your heart and give your mind to renewal through the study of His Word, through prayer, and through service, God will transform you.

The word *transform* in the original Greek language of the New Testament is *metamorphoo*, from which we get our word *metamorphosis*. It is the word we use when we are talking about a caterpillar being transformed into a butterfly (or, in this case, a rodent being transformed into an image-bearer of the Almighty God).

When Jesus said, "If any one wishes to come after Me, let him deny himself, and take up his cross and follow Me," He was not talking about a denial of your personality or some kind of ascetic self-denial. If you want to follow Jesus, you do not have to go live in a cave somewhere in the desert, wear wild-animal skins, and eat bugs. Denying yourself means denying the self-centered part of who you are. It means living your life to the fullest for the glory of God.

You may or may not be called to write hit songs, pastor a megachurch, or become a successful actor. You may or may not be called to be a mom, a mechanic, or a construction worker. But I do know this, if you end up doing any of those things, God wants you to do them full bore, with all you have and for His glory. If you are a songwriter, write the best songs you can write. If you are called to pastor, do so with a heart full of compassion. If God does want you to become an actor, a mom, a mechanic, or a construction worker, you can rest assured that God wants you to do those things with passion, integrity, diligence, and discipline. No matter what you do, will to do it for the glory of God, being all the person He has designed you to be.

In Christian spirituality, we answer all of the questions about what God wants us to *do* based on the answers to the questions about who God wants us to *be*. The Christian faith is about *being* before it is about *doing*. God wants you to know all the richness of life in the Spirit, a vibrant life, full of new growth.

In each chapter of this book, I have tried to describe how the life of the Spirit is experienced and expressed from the Christian point of view. If you find yourself wanting to learn more, please explore some of the excellent books that I have listed in the bibliography section that follows.

May God fill you with all His fullness as you continue to draw near to Him. Lean hard into His grace. God loves you. He will strengthen you, He will help you grow, and He will even supply the faith you need to believe. And remember, Christian spirituality is a lifelong process. It is all about *becoming*.

Untangling Basic Theological Terms

Agnostic—A person who believes that we cannot ultimately know the answers to our questions about spiritual issues.

Anthropomorphism—Attributing human characteristics or actions (e.g., eyes, seeing, ears, hearing, etc.) to something non-human such as God, angels, or the devil.

Apostle—An apostle is one sent on a mission. In the case of the Christian apostles, this term refers to those whom Jesus personally selected to represent Him, establish the church, and define Christian doctrine. They were eyewitnesses to the fact that Jesus had been raised from the dead, and they were charged with the mission of spreading the good news of the gospel to the world at large. There were 12 apostles appointed by Jesus from among the original disciples. After Judas betrayed Christ, he was replaced by Matthias. Paul, who had also seen the risen Christ in a vision on the road to Damascus, was also called an apostle.

Atheist—A person who denies the existence of God.

Atonement—The word means "to satisfy." As a theological term it refers to the action of Christ in reconciling mankind to God. By His death on the cross, Christ purchased our salvation and satisfied both the justice and mercy of God.

Baptism—A ceremony in which new converts to Christianity make a symbolic, public declaration of what has happened to them on a spiritual level. Baptism symbolizes the new believer's identification with Christ in both His death and resurrection. New believers declare their death to their former life and their resurrection to a new life in Christ.

Body of Christ—The analogy used by the apostle Paul to describe the mystical union of believers with Christ as our "head" and with each other as fellow members or parts of the body of Christ. It speaks of our diversity in that a body has many parts, and of our unity in that the body is still one.

Calling—A summons or directive from God, initially to turn from our sin and follow Christ, but also at times to specific works in the church or the world as servants of God.

Canon—The term used to denote the list of books generally accepted into the Bible as the authoritative Word of God. This list includes the 39 books of the Old Testament and the 27 books of the New Testament.

Catholic—Technically this term means "universal," as it is used in the Apostle's Creed. In contemporary usage it often refers to anything having to do with the Roman Catholic Church.

Confession—There are two ways in which this term can be used. First, it may describe the confession of sin in which a person acknowledges his wrongdoing and his remorse for having displeased God. Second, it can mean to declare your faith in, adherence to, or agreement with a teaching. When we confess the Apostle's Creed, we are declaring that we believe the statements of the creed to be true.

Consecration—The setting apart of people or things for the service of God.

Conversion—The combination of repentance and faith which leads someone to turn and follow Christ. The circumstances under which this happens are unique for every person who comes to follow Him.

Covenant—The agreement or promise offered by God which is designed to secure a relationship between God and humankind. Prior to Christ, God had offered the old covenant of the Law, which failed because of humanity's inability to live up to it. Now, through Christ, we have the new covenant of grace.

Creed—A summary of belief. The Christian church has adopted several, the most widely accepted of which are the Apostle's Creed and the Nicene Creed.

Cult—A group that is a deviation from true Christianity. Its followers usually display an intense loyalty to their leadership. These groups often take an unbalanced approach to interpreting Scripture, mutual accountability, and methods and forms of worship, twisting them or distorting them from their original and true meaning.

Deism—This is a term that is generally associated with a group of seventeenth-century English writers who propagated the idea that while God was responsible for the creation of the world, He is no longer involved in the affairs of His creation.

Doctrine—The body of principles which are given through teaching and instruction.

Epistemology—That branch of philosophy which deals with the origins, limits, and methods of human knowledge.

Epistle—Another term for *letters*, usually referring to the letters written by the various apostles and contained in the New Testament.

Eschatology—That part of theology which deals with the end times or last days, especially concerned with the Second Coming of Christ and the end of this present world.

Eternal life—Life without end, even when we leave this temporal world. Eternal life is the free gift of God for those who have placed their trust in Christ.

Evangelical—This term has evolved a good bit over the years but is used in a general way to refer to those who embrace the supreme authority of the Scriptures as God's Word and the atoning death of Christ as the only means of salvation.

Evangelism—A term describing any effort to convince other people of the truth of the gospel and to persuade them to become Christians.

Faith—In the Christian sense, faith means a belief and trust in God which results in a strong allegiance and loyalty to Him. The New Testament tells us that "faith is the assurance of things hoped for, the conviction of things not seen" (Hebrews 11:1).

Fall, the—The original event whereby humankind chose to willfully disobey God, which resulted in separation from God, the distortion of the image of God in humanity, the spoiling of the rest of creation, and the curse of death.

Filled with the Spirit—That ongoing experience of yielding ourselves completely to the Holy Spirit for enrichment, empowerment, and employment.

Gifts of the Spirit—The variety of special abilities given by the Holy Spirit to believers to be used for the good of the entire body of Christ. These are listed in Romans 12; 1 Corinthians 12; and Ephesians 4.

Gospel—The *good news* about how Jesus Christ has come to offer us forgiveness and eternal life through His death and resurrection. "The Gospels" refer to the first four books in the New Testament: Matthew, Mark, Luke, and John.

Grace—In Christian theology, grace is the unearned and undeserved gift of God whereby He offers forgiveness and salvation to sinners, and where God's influence works in us, giving us a new life in Christ. While *mercy* means "not getting what we deserve," *grace* means "getting something we do not deserve."

Heaven—The place where we are in the eternal presence of God and experience all the fullness of His love, joy, and peace, as well as the absence of the negative effects of the Fall (e.g., sickness, sorrow, death, etc.).

Hell—Also referred to as *Hades, Sheol,* and *Gehenna.* The place of eternal torment and separation from God.

Heresy—Teaching that departs from and contradicts established, orthodox truth.

Holy—Set apart for God and His service. We are called to be holy and to reflect the image of God in Christ.

Incarnation—The term which describes how God the Son took on flesh and became a man in the Person of Jesus Christ. This doctrine teaches that Jesus Christ was both God and man at the same time, having both a divine and a human nature.

Inspiration—The means by which God communicated to the authors of the Bible precisely what He wanted included in His Word.

Judgment—The action of God whereby He holds all people accountable for their thoughts and deeds. Both believers and unbelievers will face the final judgment of God. Believers will be declared "not guilty" because they have placed their trust in Christ and His work on the cross on their behalf.

Justification—A term which describes how a sinner is made acceptable to God as God moves that person from the status of guilty to not guilty by His grace. This is not arbitrary, but occurs when the repentant sinner places faith in Christ and His atoning work on the cross.

Law, the—This term usually refers to the Ten Commandments and/or the first five books of the Old Testament, in which God defines the patterns of behavior for His people to express their love for God and each other.

Messiah—The Hebrew term also referred to by its Greek version, *Christ.* It is the title of the One God anointed to set His people free from their sin.

Mystery—That which is beyond human understanding and explanation.

Natural theology—The general knowledge of God arrived at through human reason alone and apart from any specific divine revelation.

Omnipotent—All-powerful, able to do anything that can be done.

Omnipresent—Present everywhere at the same time.

Omniscient—All-knowing, all-wise.

Original sin—Our predisposition toward sinful thoughts and deeds.

Orthodox—Correct doctrine, true to the original idea, conforming to the established standards.

Pantheist—A person who believes that everything is an aspect of the divine. A pantheist might worship nature and believes in a kind of moral neutrality.

Polytheist—A person who believes in more than one god.

Protestant—A term referring to any member of a non-Catholic Christian church. The term comes from a sixteenth-century protest movement against Catholic doctrine and practices.

Providence—The care and guidance of God over all creation and specifically over those who have placed themselves under His care by trusting in Christ.

Redemption—The act of Christ in dying for our sins to purchase our salvation.

Reformed—An adjective which connotes ties to the teachings of the sixteenth-century reformer John Calvin.

Regeneration—The act of the Holy Spirit in which we are given a new birth to a new life in Christ.

Repentance—Having a change of mind and heart which leads to a change of behavior or attitude. Turning away from our sin and turning toward God.

Resurrection—The historical, space-time event where God raised Jesus from the dead and dismantled death forever. The significance of this event confirms the deity of Christ and offers those who place their trust in Christ assurance that this life is not the end.

Revelation—The initiative God takes to unfold or unveil information about Himself, His plans, and His purposes. Revelation makes knowledge available to us that we would otherwise have no access to, as it is simply beyond human reason and discovery. It is also the name of the last book in the New Testament.

Salvation—Also referred to as *redemption*, the act of God whereby He rescues the souls of repentant humans from the dire circumstances of punishment we are due because of our guilt and the pollution of our sin.

Sanctification—Following *justification,* sanctification is the ongoing process of renewal toward holiness in the life of the believer, accomplished by the Holy Spirit.

Theism—Belief in God.

Theology—The study of God and God's relationships with humanity and all of creation.

Trinity—The unity of God in three persons known as God the Father, God the Son, and God the Holy Spirit. The Christian view holds that while God is one in essence, God is three in personality and function.

Bibliography

Adler, Mortimer J. *Truth in Religion.* New York: Collier Books, 1990.

Benner, David. *Care of Souls: Revisioning Christian Nurture and Counsel.* Grand Rapids, MI: Baker Books, 1998.

Berkhof, Louis. *Systematic Theology.* Grand Rapids, MI: Wm. B. Eerdmans Publishing Co., 1996.

Buechner, Frederick. *The Hungering Dark.* San Francisco: HarperSanFrancisco, 1969.

Chapell, Bryan. *Christ-Centered Preaching: Redeeming the Expository Sermon.* Grand Rapids, MI: Baker Books, 1994.

Chesterton, G.K. *Orthodoxy.* New York: Image Books/Doubleday, 1959.

Clark, Kelly James. *Philosophers Who Believe.* Downer Grove, IL: InterVarsity Press, 1993.

Curtis, Brent, and Eldredge, John. *The Sacred Romance: Drawing Closer to the Heart of God.* Nashville, TN: Thomas Nelson, 1997.

Eldredge, John. *The Journey of Desire: Searching for the Life We've Only Dreamed Of.* Nashville, TN: Thomas Nelson, 2000.

Erickson, Millard J. *Christian Theology.* Grand Rapids, MI: Baker Books, 1998.

———. *Saved by Grace.* Grand Rapids, MI: William B. Eerdmans Publishing Co., 1989.

Foster, Richard. *Celebration of Discipline: The Path to Spiritual Growth.* San Francisco: Harper & Row, 1988.

Gallup, George, Jr., and Jones, Timothy. *The Next American Spirituality: Finding God in the Twenty-First Century.* Colorado Springs, CO: Victor Books, 2000.

Guinness, Os. *The Call.* Nashville, TN: Word Publishing, 1998.

Hoekema, Anthony A. *Created in God's Image.* Grand Rapids, MI: William B. Eerdmans, 1986.

Laurie, Greg. *The Upside Down Church.* Wheaton, IL: Tyndale House, 1999.

Lewis, C.S. *Mere Christianity.* New York: Macmillan Publishing, 1979.

———. *Miracles.* New York: The MacMillan Company, 1947.

———. *The Problem of Pain.* New York: Macmillan Publishing, 1962.

———. *The Screwtape Letters.* New York: The MacMillan Company, 1943.

———. *Surprised by Joy.* New York: Harcourt, Brace & World, Inc., 1955.

———. *The Weight of Glory.* New York: Macmillan Publishing, 1980.

Manning, Brennan. *The Ragamuffin Gospel: Embracing the Unconditional Love of God.* Sisters, OR: Multnomah Publishers, 1990.

———, *Ruthless Trust: The Ragamuffin's Path to God.* San Francisco: HarperSanFrancisco, 2000.

McCartney, Dan, and Clayton, Charles. *Let the Reader Understand: A Guide to Interpreting and Applying the Bible.* Wheaton, IL: Victor Books, 1994.

McDowell, Josh, and Bill Wilson. *The Best of Josh McDowell: A Ready Defense.* Nashville, TN: Thomas Nelson, Inc., 1993.

McGrath, Alister. *Christian Spirituality.* Oxford, England: Blackwell Publishers, 1999.

———. *Historical Theology.* Oxford, England: Blackwell Publishers Inc., 1998.

———. *I Believe: Exploring the Apostle's Creed.* Downers Grove, IL: InterVarsity Press, 1997.

———. *The Journey.* New York: Doubleday, 1999.

———. *Studies in Doctrine.* Grand Rapids, MI: Zondervan Publishing House, 1997.

———. *The Unknown God.* Grand Rapids, MI: William B. Eerdmans, 1999.

Meyer, F.B. *The Secret of Guidance.* Chicago: Moody Press, 1997.

Miller, Calvin. *Into the Depths of God: Where Eyes See the Invisible, Ears Hear the Inaudible, and Minds Conceive the Inconceivable.* Minneapolis, MN: Bethany House, 2000.

Moreland, J. P., and Nielsen, Kai. *Does God Exist?* Buffalo, NY: Prometheus Books, 1993.

Nash, Ronald H. *Faith and Reason.* Grand Rapids, MI: Zondervan, 1988.

Pascal, Blaise. *Pensees, The Provincial Letters.* New York: Random House, 1941.

Pinnock, Clark H. *Reason Enough.* Downers Grove, IL: InterVarsity Press, 1980.

Plantinga, Alvin C. *God, Freedom, and Evil.* Grand Rapids, MI: William B. Eerdmans Publishing Co., 1986.

Plantinga, Cornelius. *Not the Way It's Supposed to Be.* Grand Rapids, MI: William B. Eerdmans, 1995.

Sayers, Dorothy L. *Creed or Chaos?* London: Methuen & Co. Ltd., 1954.

Schaeffer, Francis A. *The God Who Is There.* Downers Grove, IL: InterVarsity Press, 1968.

———. *True Spirituality.* Wheaton, IL: Tyndale House, 1971.

Sproul, R.C.; Gerstner, John, and Lindsley, Arthur. *Classical Apologetics.* Grand Rapids, MI: The Zondervan Company, 1984.

Sproul, R.C. *Not a Chance.* Grand Rapids, MI: Baker Books, 1994.

Stott, John R.W. *The Authority of the Bible.* Downers Grove, IL: InterVarsity Press, 1974.

———. *The Cross of Christ.* Downers Grove, IL: InterVarsity Press, 1986.

Stott, John. *The Sermon on the Mount: 12 Studies for Individuals or Groups.* Downers Grove, IL: InterVarsity Press, 1978.

Strohmer, Charles. *The Gospel and the New Spirituality.* Nashville, TN: Thomas Nelson, 1996.

Tozer, A.W. *The Pursuit of God.* Camp Hill, PA: Christian Publications, 1993.

Waller, Ralph, and Ward, Benedicta. *An Introduction to Christian Spirituality.* Great Britain: Society for Promoting Christian Knowledge, 1999.

Wells, David F. *God in the Wasteland.* Grand Rapids, MI: Wm. B. Eerdmans Publishing Co., 1994.

Willard, Dallas. *The Divine Conspiracy: Rediscovering Our Hidden Life in God.* New York: HarperCollins, 1998.

———. *Hearing God: Developing a Conversational Relationship with God.* Downers Grove, IL: InterVarsity Press, 1984.

———. *The Spirit of the Disciplines: Understanding How God Changes Lives.* New York: HarperCollins, 1988.

Yaconelli, Michael. *Dangerous Wonder.* Colorado Springs, CO: NavPress, 1998.

Notes

Introduction

1. Francis Schaeffer, *The God Who Is There* (Downers Grove, IL: InterVarsity Press, 1968), pp. 145-46.

Chapter 1—What Is Spirituality?

1. Clark Pinnock, *Three Keys to Spiritual Renewal* (Minneapolis, MN: Bethany House Publishers, 1985), p. 37.

Chapter 2—Longing: Is This All There Is?

1. Chris Heath, interview with Brad Pitt, *Rolling Stone*, October 28, 1999, RS #824.
2. C.S. Lewis, "The Weight of Glory" from *They Asked for a Paper* (London: Geoffrey Bles Ltd., 1962), pp. 207-08.

Chapter 3—Belonging: Am I All Alone in the Universe?

1. As found in Luis Palau, *Healthy Habits for Spiritual Growth* (Grand Rapids, MI: Discovery House, 1994).
2. C.S. Lewis, *Mere Christianity* (New York: Macmillan, 1978), p. 54.
3. William Temple, as quoted by Rowland Croucher. Internet site: www.pastornet.net.au.
4. A.W. Tozer, *The Pursuit of God* (Camp Hill, PA: Christian Publications, 1993), p. 18.

Chapter 4—What Is the Difference Between Belief and Knowledge?

1. Blaise Pascal, *Pensées*, 265.

2. Mortimer Adler, as quoted in "Truth's Intrepid Ambassador," *Christianity Today*, November 19, 1990.

Chapter 5—How Do We Know That God Exists?

1. Blaise Pascal, *Pensées*, p. 288.
2. Nancy R. Pearcey and Charles B. Thaxton, *The Soul of Science* (Wheaton, IL: Crossway Books, 1994), p. 222.

Chapter 6—How Do We Know the Bible Is God's Word?

1. Josh McDowell and Don Stewart, *Answers to Tough Questions* (Wheaton, IL: Tyndale House, 1980).
2. John R. W. Stott, *The Authority of the Bible* (Downers Grove, IL: InterVarsity Press, 1974).

Chapter 7—Learning: How Do I Interpret and Apply the Message of the Bible?

1. F.B. Meyer, *The Secret of Guidance* (Chicago: Moody Press, 1997), p. 31.
2. John Stott, *Culture and the Bible* (Downers Grove, IL: InterVarsity Press, 1981), p. 33.
3. See the Westminster Confession of Faith, 1.7-9.
4. Some good additional in-depth resources would be a set of Bible encyclopedias like the *New International Standard Bible Encyclopedia* or the *Illustrated Bible Dictionary*. There are Bible commentaries like the *Expositor's Bible Commentary* or the *Tyndale New Testament Commentaries*. For a closer look at the original language of a passage, there are Hebrew and Greek concordances such as *Strong's Exhaustive Concordance of the Bible* and *Young's Analytical Concordance to the Bible*.

   Other extremely helpful resources are the various on-line Bible study Web sites. Some of my favorite Web sites are:

   - Bible.org (www.Bible.org)
   - Bible Gateway at bible.gospelcom.net
   - Blue Letter Bible at www.blueletterbible.org
   - Christian Classics Ethereal Library at www.ccel.org

Chapter 8—What's So Special About Jesus?

1. C.S. Lewis, *God in the Dock* (Grand Rapids, MI: William B. Eerdmans Publishing, 1970), pp. 157-58.

Chapter 10—How Should We Handle Doubt?

1. Frederick Buechner, *Wishful Thinking* (San Francisco: HarperSanFrancisco, 1973), p. 20.

Chapter 11—Why Does God Allow So Much Pain and Suffering?

1. St. Augustine, *The Problem of Free Choice*, vol. 22 of *Ancient Christian Writers* (Westminster, MD: The Newman Press, 1955), pp. 14-15.
2. C.S. Lewis, *The Problem of Pain* (New York: Macmillan Publishing Company, 1962), p. 39.
3. Anthony A. Hoekema, *Created in God's Image* (Grand Rapids, MI: William B. Eerdmans Publishing Co., 1986), pp. 136-38.
4. Dorothy Sayers, *Creed or Chaos?* (London: Methuen & Co. Ltd., 1954), p. 2.
5. See Jonah 1–4.
6. See Matthew 8:18-27.
7. Sayers, p. 38.

Chapter 12—Receiving: How Can I Experience God's Forgiveness?

1. Here I have adapted a phrase from theologian John Stott.
2. Brennan Manning, *Ruthless Trust* (New York: HarperCollins, 2000), p. 171.
3. C.S. Lewis, "On Forgiveness" from *The Weight of Glory* (New York: Macmillan, 1980).
4. Kim Thomas, *Simplicity: Finding Peace by Uncluttering Your Life* (Nashville, TN: Broadman & Holman, 1999), p. 111.

Chapter 13—Becoming: What Does It Take to Grow Spiritually?

1. F.B. Meyer, *The Secret of Guidance* (Chicago: Moody Press, 1997), p. 12.
2. Richard Foster, as quoted in Edythe Draper, *Draper's Book of Quotations for the Christian World* (Wheaton, IL: Tyndale House, 1992), p. 18.